Defending the Faith in a Messy World

Defending the Faith in a Messy World

A Christian Apologetics Primer

John Warwick Montgomery

Defending the Faith in a Messy World: A Christian Apologetics Primer

© 2017 John Warwick Montgomery

1517 Publishing
PO Box 54032
Irvine, CA 92619-4032

Cover design by Brenton Clarke Little.
Cartoons by Jonny Hawkins.

Publisher's Cataloging-In-Publication Data

Names: Montgomery, John Warwick.
Title: Defending the Faith in a Messy World: A Christian Apologetics Primer / by Dr. John W. Montgomery. Previously published as Always Be Ready: A Primer on Defending the Christian Faith
Description: Irvine, CA : 1517 Publishing, an imprint of 1517 the Legacy Project, [2018] | Includes bibliographical references and index.
Identifiers: ISBN 9781948969109 (hardcover) | ISBN 9781948969116 (softcover) | ISBN 9781948969123 (ebook)
Subjects: LCSH: Apologetics.

1517 Publishing is committed to packaging and promoting the finest content for fueling a new Lutheran Reformation. We promote the defense of the Christian faith, confessional Lutheran theology, vocation and civil courage.

Printed in the United States of America

Contents

PART 1
Some Essential Preliminaries

You don't need to be an expert.

1

Why This Primer?

A short answer (appropriate for a short book) is to show how easy it is to do apologetics responsibly.

Christian philosophers have convinced the church that only the metaphysically acute can properly defend the Christian faith, and popular apologists have done such a superficial job that many shy away from apologetics in any form.

As a "distinguished research professor of philosophy"—with more degrees than a thermometer—I therefore determined to get a bad name among my colleagues by writing what amounts to a book in the "Dummies" series: "Defending the Faith for Dummies." I did not, however, so title it, since I have greater respect for readers who recognize how important the defense of the holy Christian faith really is and how important the task is of doing it responsibly.

The excellent cartoons in the book should lighten the reader's task, and we thank the brilliant cartoonist responsible for it—Jonny Hawkins.

And we cannot resist thanking the so-called New Atheists, who—in spite of their juvenile and appallingly irrational arguments—have put issues of religious truth back into the public square. As a result, even the most politically correct among us can no longer avoid facing religious claims.

"Are you absolutely sure?"

2

Why Defend the Faith—and How?

The "why" question receives an answer of extreme brevity. The Apostle Peter declares, "Be ready always to give an answer [Greek text: *apologia*] for the faith that is within you" (1 Peter 3:15). Note that this is not a pious suggestion; it is a *command*—and it is directed to all Christian believers.

One may well wonder how, then, a vast majority of Christian churches manage to avoid entirely any attempt to defend the faith. Granted, spaghetti suppers (or, among Norwegian Lutheran congregations, Lutefisk dinners—the "piece of cod that passeth all understanding") occupy most of their leisure time, but one would think that an apostolic command would have more of an effect than questionable recreation.

Moreover, if our Lord was serious when He said, "I am the Way, the Truth, and the Life; no one comes to the Father but by Me" (John 14:6) and if the apostles were not joking when they asserted, "There is none other name under heaven by which we must be saved" (Acts 4:12), no Christian can justify ignorance of the gospel or neglect preaching and defending it in a secular world.

Note the common secular assumption that all religious decisions are simply matters of personal preference—that evidence and fact have nothing to do with one's beliefs. Here is a sad example from the pen of Norwegian detective story novelist Jo Nesbø; his hero-detective, an atheist, is in dialogue with a Salvation Army officer:

"Are you a Christian?"

"No. I'm a detective. I believe in proof."

"Which means?" . . .

"I have problems with a religion that says faith in itself is enough for a ticket to heaven. In other words, that the ideal is your ability to manipulate your own common sense to accept something your intellect rejects. It's the same model of intellectual submission that dictatorships have used throughout time, the concept of a higher reasoning without any obligation to discharge the burden of proof."

It is precisely this kind of appalling misconception of the Christian position and its justification that should compel believers to defend the faith.

So, *how* does one perform the apologetic task? Let's start with how *not* to do it. Forget your wondrous, interior blessedness such as A. H. Ackley's hymn line, "You ask me how I know He lives: He lives within my heart." The unbeliever will hardly be impressed by this, since he or she can't look inside you to determine if yours is a genuine spiritual experience—or heartburn or stomach trouble. The non-Christian, by definition, has not had a Christian experience (otherwise, he or she would not be an unbeliever). You have to present evidence *outside of yourself*—evidence that can be meaningful to the seeker. This means that apologetics is, by nature, an *objective* activity.

Also, do not fall into the trap of postmodernism in which "you tell your story and the non-Christian tells his or hers." Of course, you are going to begin with the "old, old story of Jesus and His love," since there is no point in defending something until you have made clear what it is. And you'll want to find out where the unbeliever is in his or her quest for truth. But the presentation of two contradictory worldviews leaves both parties just where they started. And because there are an infinite number of possible religions and philosophies, it is imperative to present the case for Christianity. Then, if Christianity can indeed be shown to be true, any viewpoint contradicting it must perforce be rejected at the point of contradiction.

Therefore, forget what one misguided author in the field has advocated as "humble apologetics." Yes, we want to avoid any pretense of arrogance (after all, the truth of the faith is not something *we* have brought about!), but we need to offer a compelling and decisive case for the faith once delivered to the saints.

The use of the word "case" in the preceding sentence suggests the terminology and style of argument employed by lawyers in the court-room. This is not accidental. The author is also a lawyer (and an English barrister and a French *avocat*, for that matter) and is convinced—with philosophers Stephen Toulmin and Mortimer Adler—that legal rea-soning is more helpful in solving ultimate religious issues than are metaphysical or cosmological speculations. After all, philosophers never have to come to definitive conclusions, whereas life-and-death litigation in the courts must reach verdicts. Life is very short, eternity is very long, and the religious discussions of believers and unbelievers need to be conditioned by that sobering fact.

To a hammer, everything looks like a nail.

3
But Aren't All Unbelievers Blind to Evidence?

In the conservative, Bible-believing camp, there are those who deny any point to presenting evidence on behalf of the faith to those outside it. Why? Because they note that all arguments begin with unprovable presuppositions, so the Christian has every right to start with his or hers ("the God who reveals Himself in Scripture"). And, owing to original sin, "all is yellow to the jaundiced eye" (the phrase is Cornelius Van Til's)—that is, the unbeliever will always reject evidence supporting the Christian position: he will somehow rationalize it away. The best that the apologist can do, therefore, is to critique the non-Christian alternatives. Many, but not all, of these theological "presuppositionalists" are Calvinists, holding that salvation and damnation have been decided by God in eternity—so the apologetic task does not appear to them quite as decisive as it might be otherwise.

The presuppositionalist viewpoint can be criticized on many levels. Philosophically, it is quite true that all arguments start from unprovable assumptions. But, though all presuppositions are equal, some are more equal than others! That is to say, it is far better to start with presuppositions of *method* (deductive logic and inductive method that can lead to the discovery of truth) than to begin with presuppositions of *content*—that prejudge the nature of the cosmos and cannot in principle be confirmed or disconfirmed. The Christian presuppositionalist turns out to be no different

"Before the foundations of the world God predetermined I would reject your Calvinism?"

from, for example, the Muslim presuppositionalist, the latter asserting (with no more proof than the Christian offers for his or her starting-point), "There is one god, Allah, and Mohammed is his prophet." Such religious claims need to be tested in the crucible of factual evidence.

Scripturally, the fall of man did not blow away Adam's brains or make it impossible for him to recognize the voice of God; he was able to respond to God's word even after his fall into sin (Genesis 3). Moreover, throughout the Bible, prophets and apostles—and our Lord Himself—clearly expect their audiences to respond to evidence. Take Elijah's encounter with the prophets of Baal, Paul's discourse on Mars Hill, and our Lord's healing of the paralytic—to say nothing of the force of His resurrection in convincing those who previously doubted (Thomas, for example).

It is also worth pointing out that if the non-Christian always rejects positive evidence for Christianity owing to his or her false presuppositions, why would he or she accept any of the Christian's criticisms of his or her non-Christian worldview? And finally, as previously noted, since there are an infinite number of non-Christian positions, merely showing the fallacies in one or more of them never demonstrates the truth of Christianity. If the presuppositionalist were correct, the many contradictory religious and philosophical positions would be as trains passing in the night—or, to vary the simile, as irresistible forces always meeting immovable objects.

True, one's current presuppositions, prejudices, and biases influence how one reacts to new evidence. But all education is based on the conviction that false ideas *can* be displaced by truth. Even the "Kentucky colonels" of the Deep South finally caved under the force of evidence in favor of the equality of the races—or at least their children have done so. One of the most important marks of maturity is the willingness to modify one's inadequate views in the face of contrary evidence. This truth needs to be impressed on the non-Christian as a critical part of the apologetic task.

**Religious truth is no different qualitatively
from gravity or inertia.**

4

Common Sense—or Revelation?

A disturbing fact must be faced in connection with any search for ultimates—and thus in any apologetic discussion worth the effort. It is this: because of human limitations and the vast extent of the cosmos, no amount of sincere huffing and puffing will produce a metaphysically compelling, comprehensive explanation of reality.

Archimedes correctly notes that the only way one could move the world would be by a lever whose fulcrum lay *outside* the world. Kierkegaard demonstrated in his devastating criticism of Hegelian idealism that no one could have a sufficient knowledge of history to assert that an inevitable dialectic process would ultimately reach the goal of perfect freedom. The same fallacy lay at the heart of Marx's belief that a materialistic dialectic would necessarily produce a millennial "classless society." In the realm of physics, the Heisenberg indeterminacy principle shows that the more successfully one establishes the position of a particle, the less successfully one knows its momentum, and vice versa. And the analytical philosopher Wittgenstein argued with powerful cogency that "ethics is transcendental," meaning that an absolute value system or ethic could only arise outside the world of human endeavor. A pithy summary of this fundamental truth has been provided—naturally—by Woody Allen: "Can we *know* the universe? My God, it's hard enough finding your way around in Chinatown."

The point here is that every secular attempt at "knowing the universe" will lack logical or factual necessity. The only solution, in principle, is *a transcendent revelation from outside our universe*—that is, a word from God. The Christian apologist needs to be fully aware of this limitation on what can be accomplished by even the most sincere and well-meaning unbeliever.

But can this limitation not be turned around and used against the apologist himself or herself? Does not the human inability to assert absolutes at the same time prevent any kind of effective argument for the faith? Are we not forced to accept the classical adage *finitum non capax infiniti* ("the finite is incapable of the infinite") or, even worse, Lessing's "ditch," which states that the accidental truths of history can never provide the necessary truths of reason?

Not so, for we must distinguish carefully between a transcendental revelation and *the evidence for* a transcendental revelation. We are incapable (by definition) of providing the former, but we may certainly check out the claims that such a revelation exists. If (as in Islam) no evidence is available to show that the Qur'an is in fact what it claims to be—a divine revelation—or that Mohammed was the unique prophet of Allah, we must rationally reject that religious claim. But if, let us say, there should be solid prophetic and miracle evidence to support Jesus's claim to deity, we are on entirely different ground, such that we can (and surely must) follow that evidence wherever it leads. The fact that one is incapable of building a city does not mean that one cannot follow a map to the location of such a city.

It follows that certainty in religion, including, especially, the certainty of salvation and eternal life in the presence of the God of the universe, depends squarely on a verifiable divine revelation. This must go beyond a mere acknowledgment of God's existence. One of Gary Larson's cartoons makes the point nicely: God telephones earth. "Hello? Hello? This is God! Who's this?" "Uh, this is Ernie Miller, sir." God: "Ernie who? Is this 555-1728?" "No, sir. This is 555-1782." God says, "Sorry," and hangs up. *And for the rest of his life, Ernie told his friends that he had talked with God.*

In the following chapters, we shall help the fledgling apologist to understand and present to the unbeliever the case for a divine revelation with the specific content that can save—a far cry from a cosmic telephone call to a wrong number.

PART 2

The Issues

"You have one last chance to explain yourself!"

1

God: Is Someone out There?

Sigmund Freud maintained that God is a myth: believers project the "father image" to the cosmos, naïvely believing that there is a universal Father somewhere on high. In point of fact, as we shall see, it is the atheist, not the believer in God, who is the mythmaker.

Lawyers are taught never to ask a question on cross-examination for which they do not already know the answer that the witness must provide. Consider the following series of questions that lead—inevitably—to an affirmation of God's existence:

1. Do you or does anyone else know of anything in this world that can explain itself? *The necessary answer is* no. (This book requires an appeal beyond itself to explain it—for example, recourse to an author. And the author is not self-explanatory; one must, at minimum, appeal to his parents to explain his presence, and so on.)
2. Would you agree that the world consists of all the stuff in it? *The necessary answer (since we mean by "the world" the sum total of all the stuff in it) is* yes. (Denying such would be an admission not only of a serious hole in the head, logically speaking, but probably also of the need for immediate psychiatric help.)
3. Can the world, taken as a whole, explain itself? *The necessary conclusion, based squarely on the preceding, is* no.

To explain the world, then, one must go outside or beyond it for an explanation. That is to say, one must go to a *transcendental* source—or, in ordinary language, God—to explain the universe in which we find ourselves.

Two objections may be raised to this fundamental argument (called the Contingency Argument, since a non-self-explanatory world is a *contingent* world). First, why do we need to explain the world at all? The answer is, simply, as Aristotle well put it: "Man by nature desires to know." Humans are not kumquats. The kumquat, the porpoise, and the pussycat are not compelled to, and indeed are not capable of, raising cosmic questions—but the human being is. To be indifferent to the "why" of existence is, in effect, to deny one's humanity—thereby accepting the nature of a kumquat.

A more significant objection to the Contingency Argument is the claim that it really doesn't solve anything, since one can immediately pose the question, "Where did God come from?" But here, note well, one arrives at an infinite regress—for the moment that one predicates a God-to-the-second-power to explain God, one must suppose a God-to-the-third-power to explain God-to-the-second-power, and so on forever. One necessarily falls into the trap of an infinite series: a series having no end. If it has no end, it never explains God-to-the-$(n-1)$—the next to the last God in the series—since there is actually *no* next-to-the-last item in an infinite series. It follows that God-to-the-third-power, God-to-the-second-power, God, *and the universe we started with* remain unexplained. We have been wasting our time; we would have been better off watching reruns of an old television series . . .

There are really only two choices: stopping our argument either with God (period) or with the universe in which we live. The theist does the former and the atheist the latter. Which is more sensible? There is no evidence or reason to think that God is contingent, but there is overwhelming evidence that our world is entirely so. Thus the believer in God is a realist: he or she says, "The universe looks contingent, smells contingent, and tastes contingent. I therefore conclude that it *is* contingent, requiring a transcendent explanation outside of it—namely, God."

The atheist, however, is the true mythmaker. He or she says, "Granted, the universe looks contingent, smells contingent, and tastes contingent. But against all evidence, I believe that *really, deep down, it is* self-explanatory, needing no God to explain it." Such irrationality and flying in the face of the facts would appear to confirm the psalmist's assertion: "The fool has said in his heart, there is no God" (Ps. 14:1).

The Contingency Argument is supported not only from our own experience but in all serious academic disciplines. Thus, in physics and engineering, we have the Second Law of Thermodynamics—one of the most fundamental of all scientific principles. The Second Law informs us that in any closed system (any system where energy is not being added from outside) the energy in that system continually declines in workability until—in a finite period of time—it reaches zero, or "heat death." (The energy doesn't disappear; it just becomes less and less functional. It's like a California surfer lying on a surfboard: he or she is still there but of no use to anyone.)

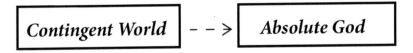

Second Law of Thermodynamics

Entropy/Heat Death

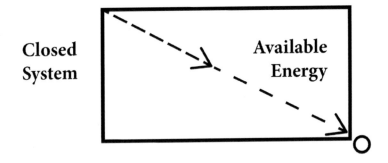

Were the atheist to be right, holding as he or she does that the uncreated universe has been around forever, it would *already have arrived at heat death*, since all finite periods are embraced in an infinite period of time. The only decent explanations for our still having the energy to discuss this question are *either* that the universe was created a finite time ago (and thus hasn't yet had time to reach heat death) *and/or* there is a God out there feeding energy in to keep the universe from going belly up (cf. Colossians 1:17). Energy, then—like everything else in a contingent universe—doesn't explain itself and requires a transcendent Creator to account for the fact that the process of increasing entropy hasn't left us all up the cosmic creek without a paddle.

Not surprisingly, therefore, Gordon Van Wylen, chair of the Physics Department at the University of Michigan and author of a leading thermodynamics textbook, states that the Second Law supports his belief in God. And the atheist who thinks about "repealing" the Second Law should ponder Sir Arthur Eddington's cautionary advice: "If someone points out to you that your pet theory of the universe is in disagreement with Maxwell's equations—then so much the worse for Maxwell's equations. If it is found to be contradicted by observation—well, these experimentalists do bungle things sometimes. But if your theory is found to be against the second law of thermodynamics I can give you no hope: there is nothing for it but to collapse in deepest humiliation."

A majority of cosmologists agree that our universe is *finite*. The Second Law of Thermodynamics, as we have just seen, supports that view. Isaac Asimov estimated the radius of the finite universe (the so-called Hubble radius) at 12 billion light years. He may have been off by a few kilometers, but the point remains the same: a universe with a radius is a universe with a diameter *and a circumference*. And a circumference means that the universe can't be all there is: there must be something (or someone) beyond it.

But can't one simply appeal, as has Stephen Hawking, to "multiverses," the notion that our universe may be just one of an infinite number of possible universes, requiring no God to explain them? Former atheistic philosopher Antony Flew called these no more than "escape routes . . . to preserve the nontheist status quo." Why? Because it in no way solves the problem. There is not a whit of empirical evidence to support a multiplicity of universes, and even if they did exist, *they* would require explanation and thus a God to account for them.

Finally, a more down-to-earth path away from atheism is available—namely, meeting God in the flesh. When asked by one of his disciples, "Show us the Father," Jesus replied, "He who has seen Me has seen the Father" (John 14:8–9). The central Christian claim is that "God was in Christ, reconciling the world unto Himself" (2 Corinthians 5:19). Let's proceed to the evidence that this is indeed the case.

"It was such a down-to-earth plan."

© 2017 Jonny Hawkins

2

Christ: Evolved Humanity
or God in the Flesh?

Believing in God is a nice idea; it solves serious philosophical problems. But it doesn't per se solve the personal problem of getting right with the universe. We are told that "the devils also believe" in God, but they remain devils (James 2:19).

The apologetic task must then focus not on abstract arguments for God's existence but on the case for Jesus Christ, who claimed to be God-in-the-flesh come to earth to provide a way of salvation for a fallen race.

Jesus presented Himself not as a simple moral teacher—a Jewish boy scout helping little old ladies across the Sea of Galilee—but as the unique Son of God and the sole Savior of the world. He claimed preexistence ("before Abraham was, I am," John 8:58); forgave sin (Mark 2:5–7); stated in unequivocal terms, as we noted above, "He who has seen Me has seen the Father" (John 14:8–9); and predicted His return at the end of time to wrap up human history (Mark 14:61–64). His religious opponents had no trouble recognizing that these were divine claims, and, in denying those claims, they condemned Him for blasphemy. Therefore, the key issue then (and now!) is, was Jesus the person He claimed to be—God incarnate—or an imposter?

Our entire knowledge of the life and ministry of Jesus derives from the documents collected in the New Testament. Thus the $64,000 question is whether these documents, and the witness statements contained therein, can be relied on to present a reliable picture of the central figure of Christianity.

Here, as in the preceding chapter, we can set out a series of propositions that—if the evidence sustains them—lead directly to a confirmation of the Christian position.

1. The New Testament documents are solid.
2. The New Testament witnesses to Jesus are eminently reliable.
3. In these documents, Jesus predicts his resurrection from the dead and the witnesses declare that He in fact conquered death.

If these assertions are sustainable, the only proper conclusion is that Jesus should be regarded as the One He claimed to be—God almighty offering the only true way of salvation.

The documents of the New Testament, when compared with the entire gamut of classical authors, turn out to be incomparably better, both in accurate transmission and in solidity of primary-source authorship. Sir Frederick Kenyon, one of the greatest twentieth-century authorities in the textual criticism of the New Testament, asserted that "the New Testament text . . . is far better attested than that of any other work of ancient literature." This means that if one wishes to discard the New Testament witness to Jesus, one can of course do so—but one must first discard virtually one's entire knowledge of classical, Greco-Roman civilization!

The authorship of the major New Testament documents is supported by external evidence that is lacking in the case of almost all secular writings of antiquity. Thus we have the claims of students of the Apostle John (Papias and Polycarp) backing up the authorship of the Gospels as deriving from either the apostles themselves (Matthew, John) or close associates of the apostles (Mark, Luke). Early dating of the Synoptic accounts of Jesus's life and ministry follows from the fact, as argued by the nineteenth-century German historian Adolf von Harnack, that Luke must have written the Book of Acts before the death of St. Paul (A.D. 64–65), and, therefore, that Luke's Gospel, written prior to Acts and together with Mark's Gospel, which was used by Luke, had to be written within a generation of the death of our Lord (between A.D. 30 and 65, a mere 35-year period).

This means that the Gospel writers' divine claims concerning Jesus were in circulation when hostile witnesses of Jesus's life and ministry were still alive—hostile witnesses who had the means, the motive, and the opportunity to refute what the Evangelists wrote had they been able to do so. That they did not can only be explained *because they could not*—there were no facts to support refutation.

The New Testament documents are also supported by solid archeological evidence. For example, the "Pilate inscription," discovered in 1961 near Caesarea Maritima, confirms the existence and political role of Pontius Pilate as set forth in the Gospel records. Also, Dr. Steven Austin analyzed the mud records of the earthquake in A.D. 33 that was referred to in the Gospels as occurring at the time of Christ's death on the Cross.

What we have, then, in the New Testament are primary-source records—accounts of Jesus from those who knew Him or from those in immediate contact with those who knew Him. Witnesses, like defendants in a court of law, are to be considered innocent until and unless proven guilty. And there is no ground for discounting the testimonies of these witnesses: they were average people who certainly knew the difference between truth and falsehood; they had no history of prevarication or psychological aberration; and they make such unadorned claims as, "We have not followed cunningly devised fables [Greek, *mythoi*, 'myths,' as in classical mythology] when we made known to you the power and coming of our Lord Jesus Christ, but were eyewitnesses of his majesty" (2 Peter 1:16).

If one applies fraud analysis to the Gospel accounts (I am a CFE, a certified fraud examiner, so I am in a strong position to do so), they come out smelling like a proverbial rose. Cressey's "fraud triangle" and Albrecht's "fraud scale" identify opportunity and situational pressure, as well as low personal integrity, as the major predictors of fraud. In the case of the Gospel witnesses, none of these apply. They (except Judas) possessed high personal integrity, had no motivation to fabricate a divine picture of Jesus—just the contrary, in light of the official religious opposition to His claims to messiahship—and, most important, had no opportunity to get away with a skewed picture of Jesus when hostile witnesses of the same events were alive and more than willing to destroy the Christian claims had they been in a position to do so.

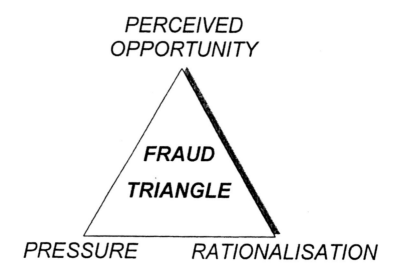

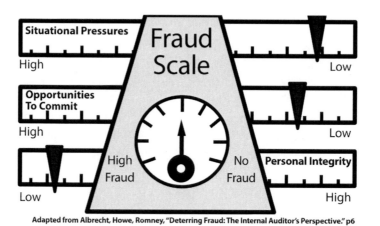

Adapted from Albrecht, Howe, Romney, "Deterring Fraud: The Internal Auditor's Perspective." p6

To be sure, if all we had in these excellent historical documents and fine testimonies were claims to divine status, the case for Christianity would fall far short of plausibility. Claims are cheap, anyone can sue in a court of law, and success depends not on claims but on proof of claims. Thus the critical factor—the factor unavailable in any other philosophical or religious context—is the evidence for the truth of Jesus's divine claims based on fulfilled prophecy and the miracles He performed. We shall deal with prophecy later;

here we are concerned with the principal attestation of Jesus's divine claims—namely, His resurrection from the dead.

The accounts of the resurrection occupy a central place in the Gospel records of Jesus's earthly life, and they are presented by the same writers who provided us with all we know of His ministry. Thus, unless we are prepared to jettison our knowledge of Jesus in general, we must view the resurrection narratives with the same respect we give to all the other information presented by those who had immediate contact with Him.

Those records make patently clear that Jesus was crucified publicly and that, during a forty-day period, He appeared physically alive to those who had known Him well—including doubters such as the Apostle Thomas. St. Paul, writing in A.D. 56, asserted that the risen Christ had appeared to a list of named witnesses—and to some five hundred others, "most of whom remain alive to the present" (1 Corinthians 15:1–8).

The only counter possible to these claims is not historical (for there is no countervailing historical evidence) but philosophical—that miracles simply do not occur or cannot be validated. David Hume's classic argument against miracles—that there is "uniform experience against the miraculous"—turns out to be perfectly circular, since (obviously) if no one has ever seen a miracle, miracles can't be asserted. (And thus the non-Christian philosopher John Earman titled his book *Hume's Abject Failure: The Argument against Miracles*.) Ours is a vast, mysterious universe in which no human being has the knowledge or perspective to pontificate on what events are impossible. The only way to find out if a miracle has occurred is to get off one's derrière and go out and check the value of the historical testimony of its occurrence. (One of the problems with professional philosophers, not so incidentally, is that they continually try to make cosmic assertions without bothering to investigate cosmic facts.)

Only historical investigation can determine whether Jesus rose. And the witness of history is decisive. If one ignores it, one can never, for example, explain the success of the Christian faith in a pagan Roman Empire replete with other religious and philosophical options, all of which fell by the wayside as Christianity, solidly based in Jesus's conquest of death, triumphed.

Three Final Considerations

But in liberal theological circles, are not the Gospel records considered the edited products of early church tradition and thus not a reliable source of information about Him? They certainly are—by the use of "higher" or "documentary" criticism. The problem with that unfortunate, unscholarly method is twofold. As we have just seen, there is powerful support for the early dating of the New Testament materials; this means that there was no time for editing, redaction, or comparable messing with the data. But, even more important, the "documentary/higher" criticism is a colossal misnomer, since there are no documents whatever to show what was allegedly edited and pasted together to produce the Gospel records as we have them. The higher criticism is entirely a *subjective* operation: the critic sees vocabulary shifts, stylistic differences, and logical movements that he or she would not have made and concludes that the Gospel writers would not have produced material of that sort. But in fact, all this shows is that the critics would not have written the New Testament as it has been written. And *that* is why God *didn't choose higher critics to write the Bible.* God, like Frank Sinatra, wanted to do it *His way.*

But why accept Jesus's explanation of His resurrection—that God raised Him from the dead? Because the one who accomplishes something, particularly if no one else can do it, is in the ideal position to explain how it happens. We prefer the successful artist's explanation of his or her work to the explanations given by critics who can't draw a satisfactory stick figure.

But why accept Jesus's divinity just because he rose from the dead? Because, as the psychoanalysts, the great littérateurs, and our own hearts tell us, death is our overarching, unsolved problem. Death can and does ruin one's whole day. If anyone can indeed conquer it, He—above all others—deserves our worship. And this, beyond all question, is through His infinite love toward us. He offers that conquest of death and eternal life to us as an unmerited gift, and that is precisely what He has done: "Because I live, you shall live also" (John 14:19).

A Final Sermonic Point

If Jesus did in fact conquer death, He is eminently worth listening to. Presumably, as God Almighty, He has forgotten more about cosmic truth than any of us will ever know.

Therefore, if He declares that salvation entails x and not y, the matter is perforce *settled*. Speculation ceases. And His message is that, owing to our endemic selfishness, we cannot save ourselves whatever we do (intellectually, socially, politically, morally, or psychologically). Salvation, He says, is available as a free gift to those who will admit their absolute need for it and who come to Him to receive His love and grace offered through His death for our sins on the Cross.

In our next two chapters, we shall see the implications of Jesus's divinity for the questions of God's nature and biblical revelation in general.

"Sure, the nature of light is an apt analogy."

3
The Trinity: Does Three Equal One?

Fundamental to the truth of the Christian faith and set forth explicitly in its historic creeds (Apostles', Nicene, and Athanasian) is the doctrine of the Holy Trinity, that God is one and exists in three persons: Father, Son, and Holy Spirit. Non-Christians—especially Unitarians and Jehovah's Witnesses—ridicule this teaching, pointing out that "1 plus 1 plus 1 does not equal 1."

Sermonic attempts to deal with the problem abound, such as pointing out that whereas $1 + 1 + 1 \neq 1$, $1 \times 1 \times 1 = 1$. The problem with such "solutions" is that purely formal, mathematical explanations cannot effectively deal with concrete, empirical questions. As Wittgenstein sagely put it, mathematics is like scaffolding: it can show us the shape of the world but not what it is made of empirically.

Nonetheless, rationality does lie on the side of affirming Trinitarian doctrine, not denying it. Let's see how this is the case.

First, Jesus Himself teaches Trinitarianism, and the events of His life confirm it. At the beginning of Jesus's ministry, the three Persons of the Godhead are explicitly referred to when John baptizes Jesus (Matthew 3:13–17). At the close of His earthly ministry, Jesus gives Trinitarian marching orders to the church: "Go, teach all nations, baptizing them in the name [*singular: one God*] of the Father and of the Son and of the Holy Spirit" (Matthew 28:19). As we have seen, Jesus demonstrates His deity by, inter alia, His resurrection from the dead. The conclusion is that, as God, He is the ideal source of information on the nature of Godhead.

True, we shall be unsuccessful in explaining how God can be monotheistic and yet exist in three Persons. But, as in science, the issue is not whether we can *explain* something, but whether it, *in fact, exists*. As we have noted, the universe is so vast and complex that humans can hardly be expected to understand its inner functioning, but we are surely capable, at least to a limited extent, of discovering whether even inexplicable phenomena do in fact exist.

Take the nature of light. If light is subjected to two different, but equally sound, experimental tests, it turns out to be *particulate* as well as *undulatory*—that is, it consists of particles and waves. The problem here is that waves are not particles and particles are not waves (particles have mass; waves do not).

What do the physicists do in the face of this fact—form two denominations (Wavists and Particleists) and fight over which is the true nature of light? Of course not. They accept the paradox and term a unit of light the "photon": a "wave–particle."

If approached by a Unitarian or Jehovah's Witness claiming that such a procedure is hopelessly irrational, they would reply, "Admittedly, we don't understand *how* this can be, but the evidence shows *that* light is of such a nature." In science, we go with the data, and if all our efforts at explanation fail, so much worse for our explanations—*not* so much worse for the data.

This is precisely the position of the historic church in regard to the nature of God. Christians have no clue as to how God can be Father, Son, and Holy Spirit. But this is precisely what Jesus—who shows Himself to be God—has declared the nature of God to be. So the church employs the word "Trinity" to describe the factual situation, just as the physicist uses the word "photon" to describe an empirical fact whose mechanism is not just unknown but also mysteriously paradoxical.

Finally, this discussion should put paid to the claim by advocates of the (nonhistorical, late) Gnostic Gospels that Trinitarianism

Science (Physics)	Theology
Nature of Light	*Nature of God*
"Photon" = Wave–Particle	"Trinity" = Father-Son-H.S.

was imported into Christian theology as late as the Council of Nicaea as a result of the deleterious influence of Greek philosophy. The Trinity is inherent to the teachings of the New Testament Gospels and reflects what Jesus Himself said about His own nature. The choice is therefore simple: either go with what God says about God or swallow the speculations about the divine offered by the nondivine.

"Professor, I do have the testimony of a few
key eyewitnesses."

4

How Reliable Is the Bible?

We have seen that the Gospel records are superlative historical documents. But the Bible consists of sixty-six books that have been considered by the church through the ages as divine revelation. Can this claim be supported?

We begin with an argument that, admittedly, does not prove the inerrancy of the Bible, but that will surely get the attention of anyone as to the unique nature of the Old and New Testaments. The argument is statistical and based on the Product Rule.

That rule declares that the statistical probability against a number of independent events occurring by chance can be calculated by a formula where, after taking an arbitrary value for one of the events, the denominator of the fraction representing the probability of that event is raised to the number of events in question ($P = 1/x^n$). Suppose, therefore, we assume that the likelihood of one prophecy of Christ's first advent coming to pass by chance is 25 percent: ¼. There are a host of such prophecies scattered throughout the Old Testament, and they are independent, appearing as they do in a variety of books written at different times. If one were to work with just 25 of these prophecies, one would raise the denominator (4) of ¼ to the twenty-fifth power ($P = 1/4^{25}$). The result is that the probability against 25 prophecies coming true by chance, if the likelihood of one of them is only 25 percent, would be *one in a thousand trillion*!

Of course, the probability of any one such prophecy coming about by chance is far less than 25 percent. Consider, by checking at your local hospital, the likelihood that "a virgin shall conceive and bear a son" (Isaiah 7:14). As the mathematician who developed this argument correctly concluded, "These prophecies were all foreseen events, in which 'holy men of God spoke as they were moved by the Holy Ghost.' The prophecies were given by revelation—divinely inspired."

The only possible ways of avoiding such a conclusion would be to assert either that the prophecies were written *after* their "fulfillments" in the life of Christ (impossible, since the Old Testament preceded the New Testament: surprise, surprise) or that the New Testament writers fudged the life of Christ to make it fit the prophecies (impossible, since we have already seen that the presence of hostile witnesses—the Jewish religious leaders who surely knew the Old Testament and were present during Jesus's earthly ministry—would never have let the Gospel writers get away with fabricating prophetic fulfillments to support Jesus's divine claims).

But now let us focus specifically on the case for the thoroughgoing reliability of the entire Bible. In dealing with salvation and the Holy Trinity, our approach has been to accept Jesus's declarations on the subject. We can generalize this principle: if God declares x to be the case, the matter is perforce settled. Thus if Jesus gave us advice on computer hardware and software, we would follow His advice in preference to repair manuals prepared by mere human beings. (The fact that He did not give us help on this point explains in part why "to err is human, to louse it up completely requires a PC.")

Following this line, we wish to know Jesus's view of the Bible. How valuable did He consider it?

Here are two preliminaries before we answer that question in detail. First, are we not engaged in circular reasoning ("I believe in Jesus because the Bible tells me so, and I believe the Bible because Jesus tells me so")? This, however, is *not* our approach. We began with the New Testament documents as *documents*—not as divine revelation. If we find in those sound historical documents that Jesus claims to be God-come-to-earth and demonstrates it by fulfilled prophecy and miracle and tells us that the entire Bible (including those New Testament documents with which we started) is divine revelation, no circularity whatever is entailed. It's like buying land for farming and later discovering oil on it: what one started with turns out to be infinitely more valuable than what one expected.

Second, we need to distinguish Old Testament from New Testament. The former was complete before Jesus's day; the latter was not produced until after His earthly life was concluded. Thus Jesus's validation of the New Testament will be different from His attestation of the Old.

As for the Old Testament, there is really no argument as to Jesus's view of it. In specific statements (Matthew 5:18, Luke 24:27, John 5:39, etc.), Jesus affirmed the total revelatory nature of the Hebrew Bible. When He cited passages that pose serious problems for modern secular man (Adam and Eve, Noah and the Flood, or Jonah), He referred to them as representing historical events, not myths or legends. During His encounter with the devil in the wilderness (Matthew 4, Mark 1, Luke 4), in response to the evil one's temptation to turn stones into bread, Jesus replied, "Man shall not live by bread alone, but by *every word* that proceeds out of the mouth of God." The devil had quoted Scripture out of context, and Jesus insists that one accept "every word" of biblical revelation.

A dean of the Harvard Divinity School once declared, "Of course Jesus believed in the inerrancy of the entire Old Testament; all the Jews of His day did. Unfortunately, He did not have the benefit of modern critical scholarship." To this, there is only one suitable reply: even granting the immense value of a Harvard degree, Jesus, by demonstrating His deity by rising from the dead, provides a rather more compelling authority for *His* view of the Old Testament.

Having descended in the previous paragraph to a mention of contemporary liberal biblical criticism, we are compelled to say a word or two about the "Kenosis theory." (For the unwashed, Kenosis is *not* a city in southern Wisconsin.) *Kenosis* is a Greek term signifying "emptying/limitation" and can be found in Philippians 2:7, where it is said that Christ, by way of His incarnation, "emptied Himself, taking the form of a servant." Liberal theologians have argued that this "emptying" resulted in Jesus being limited to the human knowledge of His time—such as the first-century, Jewish view of the inerrancy of the Old Testament.

There are, needless to say, overwhelming reasons not to accept such a viewpoint (which turns out to be a "have-your-cake-and-eat-it-too" style of theology); you can accept Jesus but not have to pay attention to what He says.

First, the Philippians passage says nothing whatever about limitations on the knowledge possessed by the incarnate Christ. The only instance where Jesus asserts His ignorance has to do with the time of His second coming (Matthew 24:36), and, in doing so, the fact that He was aware of the limits of His knowledge while on earth shows that He possessed "metaknowledge"—awareness of the extent of His incarnate knowledge. We can thus be sure that He would not have misled us by pronouncing on anything for which He lacked the necessary knowledge.

Second, if Jesus had been per se limited in knowledge owing to His incarnation, *not a single thing He said would necessarily represent divine truth; everything He said could be tainted by the human errors of His time.* The revelational nonresult would be logically comparable to the *Far Side* cartoon we reproduced at the end of Part 1: "Sorry, wrong number!"

As for the New Testament, one might imagine that Jesus could place no stamp of approval on it at all, since it did not come into existence until after His earthly ministry had been concluded. However, this is not the case, owing to the specific promises He made to His apostles. In John 14 and John 16, Jesus tells His apostles that when He returns to the Father, the Holy Spirit will come upon them, "lead them into all truth," and "bring to their remembrance all things whatsoever He had told them." (This gift was termed by the great Swiss theologian Oscar Cullmann as "total recall," and, pace the charismatics and those who want to turn the church into the "continuing incarnation of Christ in time," it was not a general gift to the church, but a gift limited to those who had been present during Jesus's earthly ministry—that is, the apostolic company [cf. Acts 1:21–26].)

On the basis of this promise from the Lord Himself, the early church collected the writings of apostles, together with the writings of the close associates of the apostles (whose work the original apostles could check for theological accuracy and faithfulness to Jesus's ministry). It was these writings that were accepted and formed the canonical New Testament.

But what of St. Paul's writings, comprising, as they do, the majority of the New Testament canon? The answer is simply that after his conversion, Paul was accepted by the original apostolic band as what he claimed to be: one "born out of due time," a unique and special apostle to the gentiles. Had Paul not been so qualified, the gift of total recall possessed by the original apostles would have meant just the opposite: his rejection. That this did not occur is solidly evidenced by Peter's declaration (2 Peter 3:15–16) that Paul's writings are properly to be classified with "the other Scriptures" (*ta graphê*—the Old Testament).

In sum, the Bible consists of the books of the Old and the New Testament as validated by our Lord Himself. Therefore, as sure as night follows day, "All Scripture is given by inspiration of God, and is profitable for doctrine, for reproof, for correction, for instruction in righteousness: that the man of God may be perfect, thoroughly furnished unto all good works" (2 Timothy 3:16–17).

An important topic, but you can win the argument and be no closer to Jesus.

5
What about Evolution?

A necessary starting point for any discussion of evolution as an argument against Christian faith is the nature of evolution.

One cannot stress too strongly that evolution is a *theory*—not a proven fact, much less an absolute certainty. (Indeed, as the analytical philosophers have been at pains to point out, no empirical fact or theory rises to the level of absolute certainty; only affirmations of deductive logic or pure mathematics—or tautologies ["all husbands are married"]—are absolutely certain, and that is because, owing to their formality, certainty is built in by definition.)

It follows from the nature of evolutionary belief as theory that the exclusion of intelligent design and antievolutionary argument from the public school and university classrooms can have its source only in closed-minded dogmatism—invincible ignorance. Ironically, the very people who (rightly) condemned the dogmatism of creationists who refused to allow evolutionary discussion in public education now commit the very same error of refusing to allow students to make their own decisions according to the weight of evidence for or against evolutionary explanations of human origins.

There are exceedingly powerful arguments contra orthodox Darwinian viewpoints. Here are just a few:

1. As stressed earlier, the Second Law of Thermodynamics insists that the universe at large is *devolving, not evolving.* The evolutionist, therefore, must somehow justify the idea that on this little planet of ours, the reverse has been

going on: things haven't been running down biologically but actually getting more and more complex.

2. Evolutionary theory is unable to explain how, contrary to all experience, species change into other species for the better (the more complex). The standard argument is that given enough time, anything can happen. But time is not a causal factor; no matter how long a birdhouse sits in one's yard, it doesn't produce a bird. And if, with enough time, anything can happen, this would surely include the possible collapse of evolutionary theory as such. Or the evolutionist appeals to "mutations," understood as sudden, unexplained leaps in biological development. But what is occurring here is word magic rather than true explanation. Compare the following: Layman: "Why do the swallows return to Capistrano at virtually the same time every year?" Scientist: "Instinct." But giving a name to something is never the same as explaining it.

3. As more than one historian of ideas has shown, the almost universal acceptance of evolutionary theory occurred as a social phenomenon in the nineteenth century, when "progress" was regarded as inevitable. Acceptance of the model was not mandated by experimental or empirical evidence but fitted perfectly into the mind-set of a Western civilization characterized by autosuggestionist Émile Coué's mantra, "Every day, in every way, I am getting better and better." (As a matter of fact, if you repeat this every day, you will not necessarily get better, but you are likely to get hoarse.)

4. As Michael Behe and others have shown, evolutionary theory is woefully inadequate as a general biological model. At the very outset of biological development, one encounters bacteria that nonetheless manifest complexity of such a nature that, if encountered in modern life, would require engineering explanations—intelligent design in spades. But there has been no time available to account for the development of such complexity on the bacterial level: we are at the very beginning of biological life.

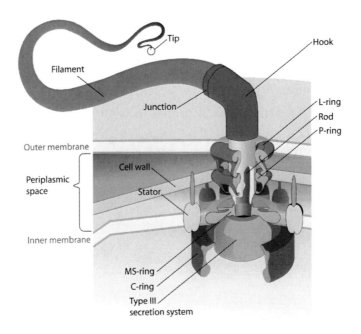

So there are strong reasons not to buy into organic evolution. But we need to be very careful as we approach this subject apologetically. There is almost universal acceptance of the evolutionary model in our secular world—and our object in apologetics is *to bring people to Christ*, not to refute false or unfortunate opinions. Therefore, let us try to think in terms of what would best constitute an apologetic approach when evolution is at issue.

If the objector uses evolution to argue that the Bible is nonrevelatory, we must of course point out that Jesus—God Almighty—held it to be revelatory, cover to cover, including the early chapters of Genesis. But this takes us immediately to the question of how the Genesis account of creation should be interpreted.

There are three major possibilities: (1) the text sets forth a literal, six-day creation; (2) the text is metaphorical, telling us *that* God created the world but not *how* He did it; (3) the text is literal except in its understanding of time periods, and we are able to correlate the order of creation events in Genesis with the appearance of biological species at long intervals in geological and biological history.

Now, if we were doing systematic theology in its dogmatics branch (setting forth the most likely doctrine derivable from a historical, grammatical understanding of the biblical text), we would doubtless choose, as has the Christian church through most of its history, option 1. After all, theology has the advantage of having its data already in propositional form, whereas science can make more slips between cup and lip owing to its having not only to collect sound data but also to arrive at sound propositional interpretations of those data.

But note that we are doing *apologetics*, not dogmatics. Our object is to get the unbeliever to the Cross of Christ, not to insist that he or she accept the best theological solution to every contested issue—particularly when that issue is not one on which his or her personal salvation necessarily depends.

Thus it is legitimate for the apologist to say something like the following:

> "Among serious Christians who believe in the entire truth—the inerrancy—of the Bible, there are different views of how to interpret Genesis. These include the three views described previously. I am not saying that I think all three are of equal value. But as long as they are represented among serious believers, one cannot refuse to consider the truth of Christianity on the ground of an alleged absolute contradiction between the Bible and science on the evolution issue. So can't we shelve the evolution question, as least for the time being, and return to the central issue of Jesus Christ, answering His question, 'Who do you say that I am?'"

The reader will, of course, wonder where this author stands personally on the matter.

I once had a fairly stormy telephone conversation with creationist Henry Morris, who said, "The greatest apologetic issue of our time is the refutation of evolution!" I replied, "Come off it, Henry. The greatest apologetic issue of our time—or any other time—is the case for Jesus Christ. Antievolution has never saved anybody. Only Jesus Christ saves."

I find option 2 the least attractive, even though it has been held by such influential theologians as Teilhard de Chardin (a Roman Catholic, and thus necessarily committed by the *Canons and Decrees of the Council of Trent* to the inerrancy of the Bible). I cannot see turning evolution into a primary theological theme. Entropy seems to me far more fundamental than progress on the biological scene—particularly in the human sphere. Our Lord did not seem to be looking forward to an evolutionary "omega point" at the climax of human history. Rather, he asked the (apparently rhetorical) question, "When the Son of man comes, will He find faith on the earth?" (Luke 18:8).

Option 3 can be very helpful with unbelievers unwilling to jettison evolutionary theory. After all, it allows for development within species but doesn't require one to affirm evolution from one species to another—for which there is inadequate evolutionary evidence anyway. It requires only a nonliteral use of the Hebrew word "day" (*yom*), and in 2 Peter 3:8, we are told that "one day is with the Lord as a thousand years, and a thousand years as one day."

In the final analysis, the strictly literal view (option 1) is entirely legitimate. Indeed, if God had preferred to create everything in six minutes, I would be the last to object. But in an era of almost universal acceptance of Darwinian and quasi-Darwinian beliefs, I am certainly not going to try to win antievolutionary arguments at the expense of losing eternal souls.

Whatever one's interpretation of the Genesis account of creation, it is imperative that we do not compromise the central biblical teaching that the first human creature *sinned*, thereby bringing the human race into a condition where "all have sinned and come short of the glory of God" (Romans 3:23). I do not think that it is important whether or not that first human had arms long enough to scratch his feet without bending over. But he must have been able to communicate with his Creator and must have refused to do God's revealed will. Otherwise, the very gospel is imperiled: if there is no First Adam, there can be no meaningful Second Adam (Romans 5).

Finally, note well that if we are successful in bringing an unbeliever to the Cross of Christ, so that he or she enters into a saving relationship with Him, the Holy Spirit will assuredly enter that individual's heart and the person will begin to look at the Bible through Christ's eyes. This will provide the most powerful motivation to take Genesis as seriously as Jesus did—a motivation far more compelling than your (or my) effort to convince a person who is not yet a Christian believer that most of contemporary biological science is seriously off base. Would not most of us, lacking doctorates in geology and/or biology, be better off moving the apologetic argument from evolution to the historical case for Jesus Christ—on which, after all, eternal salvation squarely depends?

"Pastor suggested the rhythm method."

© 2017 Jonny Hawkins

6

Sexual Issues: Isn't Christianity Out-of-Date?

Oh, boy—sex! Who says apologetics isn't fun?

However, there isn't much joy in the oft-heard claim that Christianity can't possibly be true when it opposes same-sex unions.

One thing is clear: the Bible *does* oppose homosexual activity. This is true of not only the Old Testament but even more explicitly the New Testament. Romans 1 parallels such activity with idolatry: it is the horizontal (in both senses) human equivalent of vertically setting up a false god over against the true God in heaven.

Having said this, we must recognize the difference between the *practice* of homosexuality and a homosexual *predilection*. The former is a sin against nature and nature's God; the latter is a temptation. As Luther nicely put it concerning temptation, "You cannot stop the birds from flying over your head, but you can certainly stop them from making nests in your hair." The person having homosexual tendencies has the moral responsibility not to give in to them.

But as is frequently argued by advocates for the moral neutrality of homosexuality, what if one's same-sex tendencies are genetic? Even if that were the case (and such has by no means been proven), that would hardly make such activity morally legitimate. Philosopher G. E. Moore, in his classic *Principia Ethica*, identified the "naturalistic fallacy" as the idea that you can automatically move from the *is* (the descriptive) to the *ought* (the normative). This logical error has also been termed the "sociologist's fallacy," owing to the fact that so many sociologists commit it. Thus the Kinsey Report implied that with all the extramarital activity going on, there was nothing the matter with whooping it up outside marriage. One need only reflect that the general prevalence of cheating on one's income tax hardly justifies the practice or makes it any less prosecutable.

It is said that the American Indian has a genetic proclivity toward drunkenness. Whether or not this is the case (and this author is hardly pronouncing on the matter), that would hardly make drunkenness morally right for the Indian, and it would surely not be a legal defense against drunken driving or homicide resulting from conducting a vehicle under the influence of alcohol.

In short, even if homosexuality were genetic, that would give it no moral justification whatsoever.

How is it best, then, to deal with this issue within the apologetic task? First, we need to recognize that homosexual practice is a sin no different from any other. Scripture informs us that "whosoever shall keep the whole law, and yet offend in one point, he is guilty of all" (James 2:10). We certainly do not refuse to witness to the liar, the adulterer, or the bank robber; we therefore have no ground for avoiding the homosexual or treating him or her as if that offense were the unpardonable sin. (Not so incidentally, the unpardonable sin in Scripture is the sin against the Holy Spirit—that is, refusing to accept Christ's atoning sacrifice for sin right up to the point of death—and thus forgoing God's free gift of salvation.)

Second, we need to take the time and trouble to read the literature concerning homosexuality so that we can intelligently point out its social consequences—the evils that will inevitably fall on a culture addicted to such practices. Many of these arguments are "neutral" religiously and can therefore be used effectively with the non-Christian even before he or she seriously considers Christ's claim on his or her life.

Third—and surely most important—we must not confuse law and gospel by first expecting the unbeliever to clean up his or her life before the gospel can mean anything to that person. Of course, one must recognize and repent of sin in order to come to Christ for forgiveness. But this hardly means cleaning up one's whole life by one's own efforts as a prerequisite for salvation. Luther says, "I cannot by my own reason or strength believe in Jesus Christ my Lord or come to him, but instead the Holy Spirit has called me through the gospel, enlightened me with his gifts, made me holy and kept me in the true faith."

It may well be that—as in the case of unfortunate evolutionary beliefs discussed in the previous chapter—the unbeliever in the throes of homosexuality will not be able to deal effectively with this sphere of his or her life unless and until his or her life is transformed by conversion. "If any person is in Christ, he is a new creature: old things are passed away; behold, all things are become new" (2 Corinthians 5:17).

7

How Can God Exist in a World of Misery?

Ours is surely a messy cosmos. In spite of the powerful evidence that it is the product of intelligent design, a spanner—a monkey wrench—has certainly been thrown into the works at some point.

More particularly, our world displays horrors such as apparently irrational illness and death—and the ghastly inhumanities of humans toward each other, such as in the extermination camps of the Second World War.

Atheists such as Richard Dawkins present such facts as decisive counters to the existence of an all-powerful and good God. What can be said to such an argument?

Note, first of all, that this argument does not actually support atheism, since even with the evils in the world, there could still exist a god—for example, philosopher Edgar S. Brightman's finite god (he's doing the best he can to fight evil, but he's not omnipotent) or a creator god (such as Aristotle's) who is morally indifferent to human misery. Such gods, quite obviously, have few adherents; with gods like that, most people would not bother with religion at all.

The argument from evil, therefore, is really an argument against the God of the Bible, who is *both* all-powerful *and* all-good; it's an argument against the Christian God. That being the case, the unbeliever is accepting certain facts about the biblical God (goodness, omnipotence) and then claiming that the messy state of things in this world belies the existence of such a deity.

Our initial response, then, is to require the atheist to see the full biblical picture of God rather than to characterize Him by a very

limited view of His character. After all, isn't it only fair to take someone as he or she fully is, instead of evaluating the person from a limited perspective? Doesn't God deserve that minimal courtesy?

The Bible declares that God didn't create evil; evil is the product
of His creatures' misuse of their free will. Note that free will is *uncaused
volition*—there is no way that God (or anything else) can be said to
"cause" free will to be exercised in a particular way. And evil is not a
substance that God created (like of bushel of widgets): evil (singular)
refers to the broken God-relationship that occurs when the creature
defies the Creator. The product of that evil is, to be sure, evils (plural),
which are substantive miseries (robbery, murder, and the like). Natural
evils, even when they are not the product of human incompetence or
egotism (such as the destruction of the environment), are still the consequence of sin—just as the sin of our first parents brought about the
pains of childbirth and the exhaustion entailed in economic survival
(Genesis 3:16–19). This should not seem strange to us, acquainted as we
are with the psychosomatic: the mind directly influences the health of
the body, so why should not the worst human decisions (defiance
of the Creator's will) produce the worst physical and natural results?

But the non-Christian will surely retort that even if God did not
create evil, He certainly *allows* it. As an omnipotent Creator, why did
He not simply prevent His creatures from making bad decisions or
cancel out the effects of such decision making?

The answer, in the first place, is that to do so would have been to
eliminate free will (either by creating only a good world or by eliminat-
ing the possibility of making bad choices). God is love, the Bible tells
us over and over (1 John 4:8, etc.), and free will is a correlative of love.
The parent who will not allow his or her child to make free decisions
on the specious ground that it will prevent the child from getting into
trouble will destroy the child. God's love led to His creating, not robots,
but creatures who could relate to Him and receive His love. But that
entailed the possibility of rejection, as in every human parent's realization that his or her child can disregard the best advice even though the
result may be the child's destruction. God's creatures could (and did)
refuse to follow His gracious will, and the consequences, then and now,
have been horrific.

Nonetheless, couldn't a good God at least have eliminated the
negative results of bad decisions on the part of His creatures? Hardly,

since moral decisions with no consequences lose all their moral force. If I tell my five-year-old granddaughter not to grind cigarette ash into the Persian carpet and then, whenever she tries to do so, I employ sophisticated technology always to catch every ash so that it never stains the carpet, I have reduced a moral issue to a game in which she will again and again try to stain the carpet solely to see the extent of my technological expertise.

Suppose, however, the non-Christian—now reduced to quantitative rather than qualitative argument and therefore on the philosophical ropes—pleads that God surely could at least have *reduced* the extent of the consequences of His creatures' evil decisions: the common cold, yes, but not cancer; fist fights, OK, but not world wars.

Here, Scripture is plain. Were it not for God's love and grace, our whole messy creation would have passed into nothingness (Colossians 1:17). He has sent prophets and messengers throughout history who have unambiguously informed a fallen race of His will; ultimately, He even sent His own Son. The result was that His creatures persecuted the prophets and crucified His Son. God has done everything to limit human misery, even though the misery was not of His doing. One thinks of the New York City garbage strike of a number of years ago: what would one think of those who produced the garbage screaming at the garbage man trying to clean it up, "Why aren't you doing a better job?"

And we are told that at the end of time, God's Son shall return to judge the world and create a new heaven and a new earth, where all tears shall be wiped away from our eyes (Revelation 21).

The only reasonable response of the unbeliever who comes to see the full panoply of God's loving actions in and for a fallen world should be the very opposite of criticism. As the Old Testament's Job, a classic victim of demonic evils in a fallen world, was brought to recognize, our proper role is not to criticize the God of infinite power and grace but to accept, in humble recognition of our contribution to the human mess, the salvation He freely offers us.

"This isn't Hell. It's only a branch office."

8
Hell: Only on Earth?
Heaven: Pie in the Sky?

The reality of hell is not something that demands sophisticated proof. When I was an undergraduate at Cornell University not long after the Second World War, returning service men told me, "After what I've seen, my problem is in believing in God; I have no trouble at all believing in the devil." The horrors of the Nazi death camps alone have provided glimpses into hellish experience almost beyond description.

The question, therefore, is whether cosmically—not just on earth—radical evil exists and can persist eternally.

The Bible is unequivocal on the issue, and the New Testament (often presented by religious liberals as the "sweetness and light" portion of Scripture) is far more explicit on the subject than the Old. Jesus again and again speaks of hell: the rich man who, in his ego-centricity, snubbed the poor finds himself in the nether regions and is told that a "great gulf" is fixed between hell and heaven such that there is no passage from the one to the other (Luke 16:19–31). In Mark 9:44–48, Jesus asserts the eternal nature of that punishment as "the fire that never shall be quenched, where their worm dieth not."

Does this teaching not show a fundamental immorality at the heart of Christian belief? It does not, for the following reasons:

1. Worldviews have consequences, and the worst ones have the worst consequences. The individual who believes that

he or she can engage in self-salvation is at root an egoist, believing in the one god represented by the self. That denial of the greatest of all gifts—Christ's death on the Cross for our sins—warrants the worst of all possible consequences.

2. God sends no one to hell. People arrive there by their own personal decisions. Luther rightly declared that "fallen humanity has sufficient freewill to go to hell." C. S. Lewis offers a striking parable illustrating this truth. The train to hell arrives at the infernal station. The passengers are already arguing with each other, "We're better than they are; I'm better than *x* or *y*." So groups decide to found their own cities, refusing contact with others who are saying the same thing. But these cities soon break up because their inhabitants regard themselves above their fellows. The landscape of hell thins out as one moves away from the train station, until there are, at the horizon, only single huts, each inhabited by just one individual, who mutters, "Well, *I* showed them; *I showed them*." Hell, in other words, is the product of sinful refusal to accept one's self-centeredness and the rejection of the one solution for it—offered by a gracious God without cost except to Himself, the cost of the Cross.

3. But what about those who have not heard the gospel? Are they condemned because of accidents of birth or geography? The Scriptures do not answer this question specifically, but we are told that God "desires all men to be saved and come to a knowledge of the truth" (1 Timothy 2:4). This surely means that no one will miss out on salvation unjustly. One thing is perfectly clear: a fallen race can never be saved by its good works or human effort; only a relationship with Jesus Christ, the Savior, is the way to heaven (John 14:6; Acts 4:12). Perhaps, at the moment of death, those who, through no fault of their own, have not heard the gospel—or who through prejudicial circumstances have never been able to consider the gospel seriously—will be confronted by the Christ and be able, on the knife edge between time and eternity, to accept or reject Him.

Note, however, that the unbeliever with whom you are presenting and defending Christian truth is hardly in this category! Scripture is plain that those who consciously and with full understanding (*scienter*, as the lawyers put it) reject Christ's gift of eternal life have only themselves to blame for the ghastly consequences of their rejection.

And heaven? Is the very idea not irrational?

Unbelievers such as humanist Corliss Lamont have ridiculed the notion, claiming that people living in different epochs

**"Those mansions Jesus talks about
sound like woman-killers."**

of human history with different languages could hardly enjoy fellowship in a heavenly never-never land. And how would families be reunited—would the children always remain children to satisfy their parents' relationship to them—and, since there is no marriage in heaven, how would couples be reunited, and how could a God possibly have a loving relationship with so vast a number of souls, and so on?

Mathematicians insist that if one is going to do non-Euclidian geometry, one must not expect to employ the axioms of everyday Euclidian geometry. Heaven is another dimension at least (and maybe more). Science-fiction writers have no problem conceiving of worlds vastly different from our own.

The computers of the present day achieve intellectual results so far beyond the imagination of former generations (e.g., the calculation of the value of pi to 10^{13}—over 12 trillion—digits) that it would have been considered flatly impossible by those living before the advent of the modern computer.

An infinite God is surely capable of solving the paradoxes of eternity. So it may be that in heaven we perceive others always in terms that make sense to the percipient and allow for maximum communication. A multidimensional heaven can hardly be discounted by the secularist who has no problem with antimatter and black holes.

Jesus gives us few details about the heavenly realm. At one point He says, "In My Father's house are many mansions; *if it were not so, I would have told you*" (John 14:2). The implication of that phrase seems to be that only if Jesus told us that a good thing is *not* present in heaven should we assume that it isn't there. As C. S. Lewis put it, no good thing is ever lost: Narnia is infinitely greater on the inside than one could have imagined before entering the wardrobe from the outside. One's favorite pussycat is in heaven? Why not?

But the essence of heaven is that it is God's realm—and thus a realm of perfect love. Hell is just the opposite. The unbeliever needs to understand this and determine which environment he or she would prefer for eternity.

Part 3
Decision Time

Claim ≠ Proof

1

Why Not Other Worldviews?

Christianity is hardly the only religious or philosophical option available to the seeker. How often we hear that "there are many roads up the mountain to salvation; sincerity is what really counts." So why choose Christianity in preference to one of the legion of competing claims?

The answer is simple: the alternatives do not rise above the level of claims. What is needed is *evidence and proof* to support claims—especially where eternity is in the balance.

Take philosophical/metaphysical solutions for the human dilemma. It has been noted that whereas, in the sciences, a less adequate worldview (the Ptolemaic system, for example) is eventually replaced by a more adequate cosmology (the Newtonian system) as a result of experimental evidence and greater explanatory power, in philosophy all the prior metaphysical offerings are still on the table (Platonism, Aristotelianism, Hegelian idealism, contemporary existentialism, etc.). Why is this? Because these worldviews *lack testability*. They might be true, they might be false. But who's to say?

Or consider religious options. Taoism declared that the (undefined) Tao is the meaning of all things. Of its founder, Lao-Tse, we know nothing other than what is set forth in a 248-word biographical sketch written some five hundred years after his death. The Taoist scriptures (the Tao Te Ching) contain such moralistic trivia as "Don't point at a rainbow."

Hinduism maintains that any dip in the Ganges river washes away all previous sins. At festivals such as the Kumbh Mela at

Allahabad, one's ablutions in the Ganges ensure that at death, he or she can escape the endless round of reincarnations and enter into the bliss of union with the absolute. Hinduism has never opposed the caste system; Gandhi said that it was only his contact with Christianity that led him to see its gross social evils.

Buddhism originated with Gautama, and what we know of him is virtually nil; sayings attributed to him are contained in documents written two centuries after his death. Salvation in this world and the next is supposed to come from a denial of all desire (not just desire for what is morally wrong). The absence of any meaningful ethic led Buddhists to become kamikaze pilots in World War II and, significantly, to the rejection of the Buddhist path by such Westerners as novelist Arthur Koestler. In 1995, the two-year-old son of a herdsman was proclaimed the fourteenth reincarnation of the Tibetan living Buddha; the decision was based on the finding of his name in one of the balls of barley flour dough chosen by an elimination process at the altar of a local shrine.

In Islam, we are told that "there is one God, Allah, and Mohammed is his prophet." Not a shred of evidence exists to back this up: Mohammed performed no verifiable miracles to support his claims. In Muslim tradition, there was indeed his miraculous "night journey" on a heavenly horse, but, sadly, this occurred without witnesses. (One thinks immediately of those ghosts who are never present when psychical investigators come to the haunted house to observe them.)

In defiance of the primary-source testimonies to the life and ministry of Jesus collected in the New Testament, the Qur'an declares, in the eighth century after Christ, that He never died on the Cross, was not the Son of God, and though a prophet, He did not rise to the level of the supreme and final prophet, Mohammed.

If I were to claim today, five hundred years after the discovery of America (*pace* the Vikings), that not Christopher Columbus but his uncle Alfonso discovered America, would any reputable historian spend ten minutes bothering to refute me—in the absence of any and all documentary proof?

It's easy to claim divine revelation for one's writings (I have myself thought of this possibility; think of how it would increase royalties!). But claims hardly equal proof.

And there is the sobering fact that virtually all contemporary terrorism occurs within an Islamic context and is defended by fanatical followers of the Prophet. Unlike what critics of Christianity cite as "Christian" social evils, such as the Inquisition, where the activity has in fact been conducted by "fellow travelers"—in defiance of the moral standards of Jesus, the founder of the religion—Islamic atrocities are entirely consistent with the violence of Mohammed's life and teachings and the warlike history of that religion.

Or regard the sects and the cults.

The claims of Mormonism rest on the allegedly revelatory character of the Mormon sacred writings: the Book of Mormon, the Pearl of Great Price, on so on. The Book of Mormon presents a Near Eastern origin for the indigenous American peoples; this has been thoroughly discredited by the DNA evidence of the Asian origins of American natives. The Pearl of Great Price contains the so-called Book of Abraham, which the founder of Mormonism, Joseph Smith, claimed he translated from Egyptian mummy wrappings. In point of fact, what he "translated" had nothing whatever to do with Abraham; it was a copy in hieratic script of the Sensen Papyrus, of the same genre as the Egyptian Book of the Dead. Smith even misidentified an illustration of the god Osiris as picturing Abraham on Pharaoh's throne!

Or take Scientology—L. Ron Hubbard's transmutation of science fiction into religion. Its entirely unprovable mythology teaches that Xenu, an evil prince reigning over the galactic universe, transported beings to earth to solve an overpopulation problem; their souls ("Thetans") explain the human condition today and its manifold problems. We need to become "Operating Thetans" by doing away with troublesome "Body Thetans" and our "engrams"—that is, our negative personal characteristics often acquired in previous lives. How does one achieve this? Through scientological "auditing" sessions, involving increasingly expensive counseling using the "E-meter," a kind of electronic lie detector. Operating Thetans can, inter alia, control people with their thoughts and even communicate with animals and plants. In spite of the adherence of movie idol Tom Cruise to Scientology, one is hard put to take such beliefs with any seriousness whatever. (And why should one be impressed by Tom Cruise's beliefs? Wasn't Paul Newman a far better actor?)

Now, *what do all these worldviews have in common* (and note that they are merely representative of the entire gamut of non-Christian ideologies)? The common factor is *their utter nontestability*. There is no way of confirming or disconfirming their central teachings. To quote physicist Wolfgang Pauli's comment in the margin of a colleague's paper, "This isn't right; it isn't even wrong."

Surely, in contrast with the solid historical evidence for the Deity of Jesus Christ, resurrected from the dead, no greater error is possible than accepting the unverifiable in preference to factuality. The way to heaven is offered by Christ Himself as the route to reality—in diametric contrast to paths to never-never land.

"How often have I said to you that when you have eliminated the impossible, what remains, however improbable, must be the truth."

2

Doesn't an Extraordinary Claim Require Extraordinary Evidence?

A most influential current argument against the effectiveness of religious claims based on historical evidence is represented by the late Carl Sagan's adage, "Extraordinary claims require extraordinary proof." Does not this declaration justify the rejection out of hand of all miracle claims—and in particular the resurrection of Christ? Since a miracle is maximally "extraordinary," would not the evidence required to demonstrate it have to be maximally extraordinary as well?

In a word, no! Why? In line with what we have noted earlier, the Sagan tag would have meaning if, and only if, one knew the fabric of the universe—its cosmic laws and what, therefore, can and cannot happen. But in Einsteinian, relativistic terms, no one has such knowledge, so no one can rationally determine the probabilities for or against a given event. Only factual investigation permits one to conclude that event *x* did or event *y* did not occur.

Moreover, the issue of miracle is not *how* the miracle occurs—resolving somehow the extraordinary mechanism of the unique event—but the straightforward factual question *whether or not the event happened.* As argued in a classic eighteenth-century defense of the resurrection, Thomas Sherlock's *Tryal of the Witnesses of the Resurrection of Jesus* states that "a Man rising from the Grave is an Object of Sense, and can give the same Evidence of his being alive, as any other Man in the World can give. So that a Resurrection consider'd only as a Fact to be proved by Evidence, is a plain Case; it requires no greater Ability in the Witnesses, than that they be able to distinguish between a Man dead, and a Man alive: A point, in which I believe every Man living thinks himself a Judge." Were this not the case, we would be burying the wrong people!

In our ordinary experience, one is *alive* at point A and *dead* at point B; in the case of the resurrection, one is *dead* at point A and *alive* at point B. The events occur in reverse order, *but the method of determining whether or not they occur is precisely the same.* There is nothing extraordinary about offering someone a sandwich to eat; if he or she eats it, he or she is certainly not the corpse (though the person might be the undertaker). Medical evidence is decisive that Jesus did in fact die on the Cross; following that, on the Road to Emmaus Easter morning, Jesus ate bread with His disciples (Luke 24:13–35).

Fact triumphs, as always, over philosophical speculation—giving the lie to the distinction between what is allegedly "possible because usual," and "impossible because extraordinary."

Rescue from above

3

A Push from Inside

All the preceding chapters of this Primer have focused on objective evidence, the kind of data the "tough-minded" person has every right to demand when faced with a choice of viewpoints, religious or otherwise. But even Sherlock Holmes did not characterize himself accurately when he said, "I am a brain, Watson. The rest of me is a mere appendix."

All of us are both a head and a heart. And those who have delved into the inner workings of the self—psychoanalysts such as Carl Gustav Jung, religious sociologists such as Mircea Eliade, folklorists such as Stith Thompson, and littérateurs such as J. R. R. Tolkien—have come to the common conclusion that humans possess archetypal motifs independent of cultural borrowing that tell us much about universal inner needs. Thus the dream life and the folk tales of humanity point to a realization that we are broken and estranged, needing somehow, like Humpty Dumpty, to be put back together again.

The common folktale of Sleeping Beauty is an illustration. A wicked witch, by persuading a princess to eat forbidden fruit, causes her to fall into a deathlike trance, subjecting all those around her to a similar fate. But a prophecy comes true: a prince discovers her and gives her the kiss of love. She recovers, they are wed, and she lives happily ever after.

Using Jung's terminology, love achieves a "conjunction of opposites," restoring wholeness. The folktale—like much of classical mythology—is a pale reflection of the Gospel story. The wicked witch represents the devil; the princess is the human race dead in trespasses and sin; the prince is Jesus Christ who saves by His act of love for a humanity totally incapable of saving itself; and the story's dénouement is the Marriage Supper of the Lamb and the eternal Kingdom.

If the reader resonates at all with this—and how can it be otherwise, since we are "tender-minded" as well as "tough-minded"—are we not thereby provided with still another incentive to receive the gospel of grace?

"We are reasonably certain this well-built bridge won't collapse, but until we're 100% sure, no one may cross!"

4

But as an Agnostic, Can't I Put
off the Decision for a While?

Admittedly, this Primer has presented a powerful case for the acceptance of the Christian message. But it is still but a *probabilistic* argument, not rising to the level of absolute certainty. So isn't agnosticism
really the best alternative?

First, as we have indicated, *no* factual arguments rise above
the probability level. Admittedly, religious issues are by definition
factual issues: whether there is a God, whether Christ is the One
He claimed to be, whether you need to be saved, whether there is a
heaven and a hell—all these are matters of a factual nature. A purely
formal religious viewpoint would not suffer from probability considerations but would be entirely *contentless*—and what good would a
contentless eternity be?

Second, we need to recognize that our daily lives consist of factual decision making. *All* such decisions are based on probability,
not certainty. The room in which you have chosen to sit while reading this book is the product of engineering stress formulas; there
is high probability—but not certainty—that the ceiling will hold up
until you reach the end of the book.

There is no absolute certainty that we shall not be run over while
crossing the street: remember the Roadrunner cartoons, and the
speed of the Porsche sports car. But few of us, before crossing
the street, leave on the curb that portion of ourselves corresponding
to the difference between 100 percent and the likelihood of success
(an arm? a leg?). When we take 100 percent of ourselves across the

street, the difference between the probability and the certainty of arriving safely is a matter of *faith*—not blind faith, but faith based on reasonable probability. This is all that Christian faith expects of the person seeking religious truth. "Lord, I believe; help Thou my unbelief" (Mark 9:24).

We live on the basis of probability decisions. So if we refuse to do so in the religious area, we are arbitrarily relegating that area to outer darkness—with no justification whatever for doing so. Such a relegation would suggest some kind of moral refusal to face the consequences of mature decision making: Fear of God? Fear of no longer remaining one's own deity?

Finally, note that agnosticism still involves at least one decision—*the decision not to decide*. So the real question is this: does the evidence, or lack of evidence, justify *that* decision?

Surely, if this Primer has demonstrated anything, it has shown that the case for historic, biblical Christianity is so powerful, and the arguments against it so feeble, that if one should ever be justified in making a religious decision, one is acting with eminent rationality to accept Jesus Christ—and making the worst of all possible decisions in not doing so or putting off that decision.

Life is short and unpredictable, and eternity is very long and very predictable.

"This is the promise that he [Christ] hath promised us, even eternal life" (1 John 2:24–25). "Neither death, nor life, nor angels, nor principalities, nor powers, nor things present, nor things to come, nor height, nor depth, nor any other creature, shall be able to separate us from the love of God, which is in Christ Jesus our Lord" (Romans 8:38–39).

Reading Can't Hurt

Suggested Resources

This Primer *has intentionally been written without footnotes or documentation—in contrast to the author's many other publications.* His major publisher in the United States is 1517 Publishing (1517legacy.com). Here is a list of just a few books for the serious student who wants to go deeper into the apologetics realm.

C. S. Lewis, *The Problem of Pain* (New York: Macmillan, 1975).

Chad V. Meister and K. A. Sweis, *Christian Apologetics: An Anthology of Primary Sources* (Grand Rapids, MI: Zondervan, 2012).

John Warwick Montgomery, ed., *Evidence for Faith: Deciding the God Question* (Plano, TX: Probe, 1991).

John Warwick Montgomery, *Faith Founded on Fact* (Nashville, TN: Thomas Nelson, 1978).

———, *Giant in Chains* (Milton Keynes, England: Nelson Word, 1994).

———, *God's Inerrant Word* (Edmonton, Alberta: Canadian Institute for Law, Theology and Public Policy, 1974).

———, *History, Law and Christianity* (Irvine, CA: NRP Books, 2015).

———, *Human Rights and Human Dignity* (Edmonton, Alberta: Canadian Institute for Law, Theology and Public Policy, 1995).

———, *Jurisprudence: A Book of Readings* (Strasbourg, France: International Scholarly Publishers, 1974).

———, *Myth, Allegory and Gospel* (Minneapolis, MN: Bethany, 1974).

———, *Tractatus Logico-Theologicus* (5th ed. Bonn: Verlag für Kultur und Wissenschaft, 2013).

Wilbur M. Smith, *Therefore Stand* (Boston: W. A. Wilde, 1945).

How Much Evidence to Justify Religious Conversion?

Some Thoughts on Burden and Standard of Proof vis-à-vis Christian Commitment

A simple answer to the question posed in the title of this essay would be "None," since it is perfectly possible to make a genuine religious commitment, even to Christianity, without troubling oneself with matters of proof. One thinks of John Wesley, appropriately to become one of the fathers of eighteenth-century revivalism and the Great Awakening, who, at a little Moravian meeting in Aldersgate, found his heart "strangely warmed."[1] Since the essence of Christian commitment is personal recognition that one has fallen short of God's perfect standards and that restoration to fellowship with Him is available only through the redemption Christ accomplished on the Cross, that commitment can occur without agonies over evidential considerations.

---

[1] "In the evening I went very unwillingly to a society in Aldersgate Street, where one was reading Luther's preface to the Epistle to the Romans. About a quarter before nine, while the leader was describing the change which God works in the heart through faith in Christ, I felt my heart strangely warmed. I felt I did trust in Christ alone for salvation; and an assurance was given me that He had taken away **my** sins, even **mine**, and saved **me** from the law of sin and death" (*Journal* of John Wesley, May 24, 1738, Christian Classics Ethereal Library https://www.ccel.org/ccel/wesley/journal.vi.ii.xvi.html).

However, in a secular age highly critical of Christian claims and offering a plethora of religious and philosophical options, many seeking persons hesitate to commit to the Christian gospel on the ground of their doubts as to what would constitute a reasonable decision. Having heard, pondered, and seen the value of what the New Testament describes as the "many infallible proofs"[2] of Christian truth, they are still deeply troubled as whether any such evidences would really justify a life commitment. For example, a participant at the July 2011 session of our annual International Academy of Apologetics, Evangelism and Human Rights,[3] wrote to us on registering, "I think Christianity hasn't met its burden of proof. I'm pretty familiar with the standard apologetic arguments, and I don't find them compelling. They strike me as useful only if someone has a preconception that needs to be supported."

This paper will deal only incidentally with specific Christian evidences as such, since these have been set out in great detail elsewhere.[4] Our purpose here is simply to pose the following question: *given that evidence for a religious position does exist*, what in principle would constitute adequate ground for committing oneself to the truth of the faith to which that evidence points?

The Academy participant just quoted uses the expression "burden of proof." This is quite natural, since evidential questions are particularly within the province of the law. We shall therefore begin in that realm—where the most intransigent conflicts of society are arbitrated by the refined standards of legal evidence. Any aid offered from a jurisprudential standpoint should therefore be of more than routine utility as we go on to treat the religious issue as such.[5]

---

[2] Acts 1:3.

[3] http://www.apologeticsacademy.eu

[4] For example, see such works by the present author as *Tractatus Logico-Theologicus* (4th ed.; Bonn, Germany: Verlag für Kultur und Wissenschaft, 2009); available from www.1517legacy.com.

[5] "If sceptics admit that the law courts are reliable instruments of justice, then they should also admit that the cognitive faculties, given adequate development and attentiveness, are reliable instruments for apprehending the world" (William C. Davis, *Thomas Reid's Ethics: Moral Epistemology on Legal Foundations* [London: Continuum, 2006], 62). For more detail on the value

Burden of Proof

What does "burden of proof" mean? In the Anglo-American common-law tradition, it refers to one of two interrelated notions: the burden of producing evidence and the burden of persuasion.

> The burden of producing evidence on an issue means the liability to an adverse ruling (generally a finding or directed verdict) if evidence on the issue has not been produced. It is usually cast first upon the party who has pleaded the existence of the fact. . . .
>
> In most cases, the party who has the burden of pleading a fact will have the burdens of producing evidence and of persuading the jury of its existence as well.[6]

One should not conclude that the plaintiff (or the prosecutor in criminal cases) always retains the burden of producing evidence. If the defendant offers an affirmative defense (insanity, for example), that defendant has the burden of providing evidence to support his or her contention.

As for the burden of persuasion, it "becomes a critical factor only if the parties have sustained their burdens of producing evidence and only when all of the evidence has been introduced. . . . The jury must be told that if the party having the burden of persuasion has failed to satisfy that burden, the issue is to be decided against that party."[7]

The interlocking of the two legal meanings of burden of proof should be obvious. In the most general terms, "traditional legal commentary has been comfortable placing burdens on the party seeking the law's intervention: on the plaintiff in civil cases and on the prosecution in criminal trials."[8] This is based on common sense, as

---

of legal evidence to the defense of Christian truth, see John Warwick Montgomery, *History, Law and Christianity* (Calgary, Alberta: Canadian Institute for Law, Theology and Public Policy, 2002).

[6] John William Strong, ed., *McCormick on Evidence*, vol. 2 (4th ed., St. Paul, MN: West, 1992), 425, 427 (sec. 336, 337).

[7] *Ibid.* 426 (sec. 336).

[8] Richard H. Gaskins, *Burdens of Proof in Modern Discourse* (New Haven, CT: Yale University Press, 1992), 23.

the great twentieth-century authority on the law of evidence, John Henry Wigmore, argued, the principle is but a special case of "the situation common to all cases of attempted persuasion, whether in the market, the home, or the forum. . . . It is the *desire to have actions taken* that is important. In the affairs of life there is a penalty for not sustaining the burden of proof."[9]

What, then, of the oft-heard claim by religious believers—especially those of dogmatic or pietistic persuasion—that "the burden rests on the unbeliever to show that the faith is *not* true"? This argument is sometimes buttressed by Scripture passages such as "The fool hath said in his heart, there is no God" (and thus, the passage is said to mean, since all people other than fools believe in God, it must be the nonbeliever's responsibility to demonstrate his or her atheism/unbelief). But (1) the text here refers specifically to the "heart," not the "head" (there may well be nonfoolish arguments against the faith even though the heart longs for God); (2) in a pluralistic world, there are numerous conflicting religious options available, so it seems silly and unproductive to expect the unbeliever to refute them all; and (3) considering the contingent nature of the universe, a cosmic negative can never be proven anyway, so attempts along this line hardly establish the validity of all or any positive propositions (such as that a given Deity exists).

Against this effort to place the burden of proof on the unbeliever, philosopher Antony Flew argued that it should rest on the one advocating a religious position: "If it is to be established that there is a God, then we have to have good grounds for believing that this is indeed so. Until and unless some such grounds are produced we have literally no reason at all for believing; and in that situation the only reasonable posture must be that of either the negative atheist or the agnostic. So the onus of proof has to rest on the proposition [of theism]."[10]

---

[9] John Henry Wigmore, *Evidence in Trials at Common Law*, vol. 9, ed. James H. Chadbourn (rev. ed., Boston, MA: Little, Brown, 1981–1985), 285–86 (sec. 2485); the italics are Wigmore's.

[10] Antony Flew, *The Presumption of Atheism: God, Freedom and Immortality* (Buffalo, NY: Prometheus, 1984), 22. Before his death in 2010, Flew moved from atheism to deism, primarily as a result of the evidence for intelligent design in the universe.

We must concur. And we view with grave suspicion the level of spirituality of believers who try to cast the burden of proof on the non-Christian. Have they never understood St. Paul's missionary principle that it is the believer who has the burden—the burden to become "all things to all men, that by all means some may be saved; and this for the gospel's sake."[11]

Standard of Proof

It should now be plain that even though our objector writes, "I think Christianity hasn't met its burden of proof," what he or she is really concerned about is not the *burden* (which Christianity properly should assume) but the *standard* of proof—that is, the degree of evidential force proffered on behalf of the faith.

What are the common-law legal principles relating to the standard of proof?

First, proof depends on *probability*, not on absolute certainty or on mere possibility. The Federal Rules of Evidence put this in very clear terms: relevant evidence is "evidence having any tendency to make the existence of any fact that is of consequence to the determination of the action more probable or less probable than it would be without the evidence."[12] This reliance on probability, rather than on absolute certainty or possibility, is fully in accord with the conclusions of modern analytical epistemology. The only absolute certainties are those created by definition (conformity to the primitives, chiefly the law of noncontradiction, in formal logic; conformity to the axiom set in pure mathematics; or self-referential assertions such as the tautology), and these operate only in the realm of the purely *formal*. Where matters of fact are concerned—as in legal disputes, but also in the religious assertions of historic Christianity—claims can be vindicated only by way of evidential probability. As to possibilities, they can hardly be the basis of decision making, since, in a contingent universe, *anything* is theoretically possible, so possibility

---

[11] Paul's entire argument is worth contemplating (1 Corinthians 9: 19–23).

[12] *Fed. R. Evid.* 401. Cf. John Warwick Montgomery, *Law and Gospel* (2d. ed.; Calgary, Alberta: Canadian Institute for Law, Theology and Public Policy, 1994), sec. 16 ("The Law of Evidence"), 34–37.

reasoning can yield an infinite number of results, no one of which is necessarily compelling.

But the law does not rest with the general category of probability; it endeavors to distinguish varieties, or standards, of probability decisions. In classic English law, two such standards exist: the higher standard applicable to criminal trials (which are the most serious, since penalties can involve incarceration, and, in America, execution) and a lesser standard for civil actions. The former standard is that of "moral certainty, beyond reasonable doubt" and the latter, "preponderance of evidence." The civil standard, applicable where only money or property is usually at stake, is a mere weighing of evidence: the party able to show 51 percent versus the other party's 49 percent prevails. In criminal trials, *moral* certainty (note that the standard is not *absolute* certainty) is required before judging the defendant guilty, and "beyond reasonable doubt" is understood generally to mean that the jury, in order to find the defendant guilty, must be able to exclude any and all other "reasonable" explanations of the crime (i.e., explanations that would fit the admissible evidence in the case) other than that the defendant committed the crime.[13]

To be sure, these two standards are not the only ones possible. "Three standards of proof appear to be recognized in the United States, proof by 'clear, strong and cogent' evidence lying midway between proof on a preponderance of probability and proof beyond reasonable doubt."[14]

At which of these levels should evidence be required for religious commitment? The best analogy would seem to be with the criminal standard, since a religious decision, like verdicts and judgments in criminal trials, entails the most serious of consequences, touching life itself. Defenders of historic Christianity have been at pains to show,

---

[13] In modern English law, however, the judge is not permitted to define "moral certainty, beyond reasonable doubt" beyond telling the jury that they must be "certain" or "sure" of the defendant's guilt. We have suggested in a scholarly legal article on the subject that this reticence may stem at least in part from the endemic fear of the English to offend through speaking with too much precision; see John Warwick Montgomery, "The Criminal Standard of Proof," *New Law Journal* 148 (1998): 582–85.

[14] Rupert Cross, *Evidence* (5th ed.; London: Butterworths, 1979), 118.

for example, that (1) the prophecies of the Old Testament fulfilled in the earthly life of Jesus rise to a level of statistical significance making naturalistic explanations utterly inadequate[15] and (2) the case for the *de facto* physical resurrection of Christ from the dead is so powerful that all attempts to explain it away simply do not wash: they fly in the face of the relevant (and overwhelming) historical evidence.[16]

"Extraordinary Claims Require Extraordinary Proof"?

But when one passes into the realm of religious commitment, does one not face insuperable problems not to be found in the legal realm—since religious decisions are of an eternal dimension? Can the unbeliever not argue that it is simply impossible in principle for evidence—any evidence—to justify religious commitment?

Historically, this style of argument has been presented in different guises. Going back to late classical times is the axiom, "the finite is not capable of the infinite":[17] the world is incapable of the presence of the absolute, so no amount of evidence could ever demonstrate the presence of the infinite in our finite world. The fallacy of this argument (applicable not only to a divine Incarnation and an infallible Bible but also to the real presence of Christ in the Holy Eucharist) is simply that, *qua* human beings, we have no idea what God is or is not capable of, so we have no business ruling out events a *priori*. It may well be that the reverse of the aphorism is true: *infinitum capax finiti*! Only a factual investigation of the world to see if God has entered it will ever answer the question.

---

[15] John Warwick Montgomery, "Prophecy, Eschatology and Apologetics," in *Christ Our Advocate* (Bonn, Germany: Verlag für Kultur und Wissenschaft, 2002), 255–65; also in David W. Baker, ed., *Looking into the Future* (Grand Rapids, MI: Baker Academic, 2001), 362–70.

[16] Montgomery, *Tractatus Logico-Theologicus* (4th ed.; Bonn, Germany: Verlag für Kultur und Wissenschaft, 2009), prop. 3.1–3.7; John Warwick Montgomery, *Christ as Centre and Circumference* (Bonn, Germany: Verlag für Kultur und Wissenschaft, 2011), pt. 4, chap. 2.

[17] Cf. Peter Bruns, "Finitum non capax infiniti: Ein antiochenisches Axiom in der Inkarnationslehre Babais des Großen († nach 628)," *Oriens Christianus* 83 (1999), 46–71.

Then there is Lessing's "ditch": the claim that the accidental facts of history can never attain or justify the absolute truths of reason. Here, a serious category mistake has been made. If the "absolute truths of reason" are purely formal and lacking entirely in content, then they have nothing to do with Christian religious claims at all. If, however, they are factual in nature, then only factual investigation and probability reasoning could justify them. But this is exactly what historical proof consists of: probable evidence for historical occurrences. If, for example, God became man in Jesus Christ, that contention is as capable of historical investigation as are any other purported occurrences.

David Hume argued that no miracle could ever be demonstrated, since (on the basis of "uniform experience") it would always be more miraculous that one claiming a miracle or providing evidence for it was not deceiving or deceived than that the miracle actually happened. Miracle arguments (such as the case for the resurrection of Christ) are therefore impossible from the outset. But Hume's position has been thoroughly refuted—and not just by Christian philosophers.[18] The intractable problem with Hume's argument is that it is perfectly circular: *to be sure*, if nature is completely uniform (i.e., if natural laws are never broken), miracles do not occur. *But that is precisely the question requiring an answer!* And the only way properly to respond is by engaging in serious factual investigation of given miracle claims. One cannot short-circuit the miracles issue by *a priori* pontifications about the nature of the universe. Indeed, as noted, in an Einsteinian, relativistic universe, no event can be excluded on principle: everything is subject to empirical investigation.[19]

But the most influential current argument against the effectiveness of religious claims based on historical evidence is that represented by the adage, "Extraordinary claims require extraordinary

---

[18] John Earman, *Hume's Abject Failure: The Argument against Miracles* (New York: Oxford University Press, 2000).

[19] Antony Flew's preference for a "psychological miracle" (the disciples proclaiming the resurrection and dying for it while knowing that it never occurred) over a factual, physical "biological miracle" (Christ's resurrection) is but a variation on the Humean argument and suffers from exactly the same aprioristic fallacy. See John Warwick Montgomery, *Faith Founded on Fact* (Nashville, TN: Thomas Nelson, 1978), 52–58.

proof," a saying popularized by the late Carl Sagan but which apparently originated with sociologist Marcello Truzzi.[20] Does not this declaration constitute an obvious truth militating against all miracle claims, and in particular the resurrection of Christ? Since a miracle is maximally "extraordinary," would not the evidence required to demonstrate it have to be maximally extraordinary as well?

In a word, the answer is no! Why? In line with what we have previously noted, the Truzzi-Sagan tag would have meaning if, and only if, one knew the fabric of the universe—its cosmic laws and therefore what can and cannot happen. But in Einsteinian, relativistic terms, no one has such knowledge, so no one can rationally determine the probabilities for or against a given event. Only factual investigation permits one to conclude that an event x did occur or an event y did not.

Does not the law, however, recognize a difference in the weight to be afforded to evidence in the case of less probable events? In an oft-quoted judgment, Lord Denning spoke of "degrees of proof" within both the criminal and the civil standards of proof: "The degree depends on the subject-matter. A civil court, when considering a charge of fraud, will naturally require for itself a higher degree of probability than that which it would require when asking if negligence is established. It does not adopt so high a degree as a criminal court, even when it is considering a charge of a criminal nature; but still it does require a degree of probability which is commensurate with the occasion."[21]

Here we must distinguish the descriptive from the normative. Though the variation described by Denning LJ doubtless occurs in practice, especially when lay juries are the triers of fact, the notion that the "subject-matter" should be allowed to cause a relaxation or an augmentation of the standard of proof is a very dangerous idea. For example, should a court take an easy view of the proof required if only £100 is fraudulently converted but a very tough approach to the evidence if the amount is £5,000? No one would rationally agree to a sliding evidence scale dependent on the monetary sum involved—nor should such a scale be created in relation to the type

---

[20] See John Warwick Montgomery, "Apologetics Insights from the Thought of I. J. Good," *Philosophia Christi* 13 (2011), 203–12

[21] *Bater v. Bater*, [1951] P. 35, 36–37.

of offense (little evidence to show shoplifting, much evidence to show carjacking, etc.). Thus, in discussing the standard of proof in tort actions for libel, Professor Kiralfy quite rightly observes that "the defendant who pleads justification does not have to discharge a heavier burden of proof of [the] truth of an imputation just because the imputation is a very damaging one."[22]

The application to religious arguments based on the factuality of historical events should be obvious. Of course, the resurrection of Christ is of immensely more significance than Caesar's crossing of the Rubicon, but the standards required to show that the one occurred are no different from those employed in establishing the other. If "importance" were to be allowed as a criterion for the sufficiency of evidence, it would follow that a French person could legitimately require far more evidence to show that Napoleon lost at Waterloo than would be demanded by a Japanese person—since the battle and its outcome are far less important to a Japanese person than to a French person.

But what about the very concept of a "miracle"? Is not the notion in itself so extraordinary that no amount of evidence could properly count to prove it? Here we must distinguish *mechanism* from *factuality*. The mechanism of a miracle is indeed beyond our ken, but that is irrelevant to whether or not such an event occurs. As long ago as the eighteenth century, Thomas Sherlock, master of London's Temple Church and pastor to barristers, noted that the case for the resurrection of Jesus Christ does not depend on our comprehension of how resurrections occur but squarely on whether there is sufficient evidence that Jesus died on the Cross and that following His death He showed Himself physically alive to sound witnesses.[23] There is thus nothing "extraordinary" about determining that Jesus rose from the dead: one need only show (a) that He died and (b) that

---

[22] Albert Kiralfy, *The Burden of Proof* (Abingdon, UK: Professional, 1987), 89. Professor Kiralfy refers to the case of *Lawrence v. Chester Chronicle*, [1986] 2 C.L. 329.

[23] Thomas Sherlock's *Tryal of the Witnesses of the Resurrection of Jesus* (London: J. Roberts, 1729); Sherlock's book is photolithographically reproduced in John Warwick Montgomery, ed., *Jurisprudence: A Book of Readings* (rev. ed.; Strasbourg: International Scholarly Publishers, 1980).

later He was physically alive—determinations that we make every day (though in reverse order).

Are we saying that miracle evidence should be accepted as readily as nonmiracle evidence? Are the visions of Fatima and the appearance of the Angel Moroni to Joseph Smith on the same basis as Lincoln's assassination and Hitler's *Anschluss*? We are saying simply that the standard of proof does not depend on the frequency of the event (since *all* historical events are unique) or on the characterization of the event as "miraculous" or "nonmiraculous." The standard of proof depends, in *all* instances, on the quality of the evidence on behalf of the claimed event—that and *nothing more*, that and *nothing less*. If one were to claim that a peach can be miraculously turned into a kumquat, he or she would have to show, by ordinary scientific means, that there is a peach present at the outset, and then, afterward, a kumquat. For a resurrection from the dead, the same kind of testimony is required as for any other historical event—in this instance, that the object of the miracle was in fact dead and then, afterward, physically alive. The issue of proof is not in any way metaphysical: one relies on sound historical investigation of the testimony to miracle claims of past events (or sound contemporary scientific investigation, in the case of the peach). The nature of the claim determines the method of proof, and the standard will be that appropriate to parallel determinations in the same realm.

The Existential Factor

There is, however, a further consideration worthy of treatment where religious commitment is in question. The following discussion may seem to be a variation on Pascal's Wager, but in fact it differs considerably from it. Pascal's Wager (as Pascal intended it) was an attention-focusing argument along the following line: even if there were no evidence for Christianity—or if the evidence were equally balanced *pro* and *con*—you should still accept Christ.[24] What

---

[24] Note—as is seldom recognized—Pascal, having set forth the Wager, then proceeded to show that there are, in fact, powerful arguments in favor of Christian truth. See the classic edition of Pascal's *Pensées* (H. F. Stewart, ed., *Pascal's Apology for Religion*, [Cambridge: Cambridge University Press, 1942])

we shall be suggesting here is that if (as is the case) there is good evidence for Christ's claims and therefore for commitment to Him, hesitation should be considerably lessened by the very nature of the Christian claim itself.

Suppose one is offered an Internet deal with considerable solid backup (but by no means 100 percent certainty). If one must provide a nonreturnable sum of, say, $500, one can and should be wary. But suppose there is no requirement of a deposit: one need only send in one's address (to be on the safe side, one's post office box address) and the indicated amount will be mailed in the form of a check. In the latter case, any misgivings as to the standard of proof would be resolved by the nature of the offer. One would, of course, have to have sufficient confidence in the offeror to cash the check when it arrived, but that would involve no loss to the offeree, and therefore the reasonable solution would be to enter into the transaction.

Religions differ greatly in character. The word "religion" derives from the Latin *religio*—which is a "binding." All the religions of the world other than Christianity "bind": they involve a plethora of moral, ceremonial, and social obligations. The Christian gospel, however, is—as someone has put it—the *easiest* and the *hardest* religion in the world. It is the easiest because everything for salvation has been done by God Himself through Christ, so one need only accept the free gift, but it is the hardest since this requires that one recognize one's self-centeredness and thus one's incapacity to save oneself. The hard part does not consist of having to satisfy an onerous lifestyle; it merely demands giving up one's unrealistic egocentrism—the root source of one's problems in the first place.[25]

If one considers committing oneself to the religion of Islam, questions or standards of proof are of no consequence, as the belief

---

and the recent analysis of the Wager by Jeff Jordan, *Pascal's Wager: Pragmatic Arguments and Belief in God* (New York: Oxford University Press, 2006).

[25] But what about the inevitable, postconversion "conformity to Christ"? This occurs naturally, not onerously, since (1) the Holy Spirit, who enters the heart on regeneration, is the active agent in achieving a holy life, and (2) one's value system and desires change, owing to the new love relationship with Christ—just as, after an ideal marital union, the husband will prefer to spend time with his wife rather than drink at the club with his old cronies.

system is predestinarian and deterministic; one must simply accept the revelational authority of the Qur'an without question or evidence. On acceptance, one is saddled with a social and legal code embracing all aspects of life. Even if a proper standard of proof were minimally satisfied, one would need to consider commitment most seriously in light of the obligations following on acceptance.[26]

To become a Jehovah's Witness requires a refusal to salute the flag, to engage in military service, or to employ blood transfusions even in the case of life-threatening illness. Thus, even if there were strong evidence on behalf of the Watchtower Society's Arian view of Jesus and odd exegesis of Biblical passages (which there is not[27]), one might well hesitate to commit to that religious position.

In the case of historic Christianity, however, the burden of proof is properly assumed by the adherent, not passed off on the unbeliever, and the standard of proof is the highest: to a moral certainty. If one still hesitates becoming a Christian, perhaps one should consider that *nothing* is demanded but the recognition of one's self-centered condition (attested not just by Biblical teaching but by secular psychoanalysis, the great literature of the world, and one's own degree of self-knowledge), and a concomitant admission that one cannot pull oneself up to heaven by one's own bootstraps.

Moreover, suppose that the potential and demonstrable benefits of a religious commitment are of the highest standard. This would then provide a further reason to commit where a properly high standard of proof is satisfied. In Islam, a paradise with virgins is offered, but this kind of "eschatological verification"[28] is hardly persuasive in this world. As for life in this world, it is ruled by a strict, predestinarian deity, whose decisions are unfathomable and to which one must submit in all instances (the word "Islam" means "submission"). As for biblical Christianity,

---

[26] Cf. William F. Campbell, *The Qur'an and the Bible in the Light of History and Science* (Upper Darby, PA: Middle East Resources, 1986).

[27] See, *inter alia*, Walter R. Martin, *The Kingdom of the Cults* (rev. ed.; Minneapolis, MN: Bethany, 1985); we recommend that readers use the editions of this classic prepared by the author before his death.

[28] Liberal theologian John Hick coined the term and seriously advocated it as an argument for Christianity; its silliness is reflected in Hick's later departure from the faith.

the contrast could not be greater: there is the unqualified promise to believers in Romans 8:28 that "all things work for good" on the basis of God's character as a loving Father, a promise that has been experientially and personally verified again and again in the lives of believers.[29]

Let us express this point in a formulaic as well as in a diagrammatic fashion.

Assuming that the standard of proof is satisfied (and *only* if that is the case), if one still hesitates in making a religious commitment, then where C = legitimate commitment, B = concrete, empirical benefits promised by the faith, and E = entrance requirements to the faith,

$$C = B \,/\, E$$

Ergo: *The fewer the entrance requirements and the greater the benefits, the more reason exists to commit to the evidence for a faith position already satisfying a high standard of proof.*

Or,

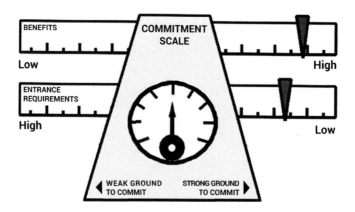

---

[29] And it is worth noting that the biblical promise of eternal life, unlike eschatological hopes in other religions, is grounded in the evidence for the de facto conquest of death by Jesus Christ. He said, "Because I live, you shall live also" (John 14:19).

We are arguing that, in contrast with competing religious claims, acceptance of the gospel is a win-win situation. Any doubts as to satisfying the standard of proof (and can this really be a problem, since the evidence level accords with the highest legal standard?) should be resolved in favor of the gospel, not against it. To argue in any other fashion is simply to declare that *regardless of the evidence, and regardless of the maximal potential benefits available with minimal demands upon me,*[30] I prefer to remain the center—the god—of my own life and universe. But that, as C. S. Lewis rightly observed, is the very definition of hell.

The conclusion is that in light of the weight of the evidence, the only reasonable course of action is that of St. Augustine in the fifth century, followed by a host of converts to Christianity across the centuries. After years of intellectual struggle, Augustine saw that Christian faith deserved his commitment. Only a moral problem remained: a lifestyle incompatible with the love of Christ. Finally, as he heard the Scriptural message "Put ye on the Lord Jesus Christ and make not provision for the flesh" (Romans 13:13–14), "by a light as it were of serenity infused into my heart, all the darkness of doubt vanished away."[31]

---

[30] The words of the gospel song are, "Just as I am, without one plea, but that thy blood was shed for me, and that thou bidd'st me come to thee, O Lamb of God, I come, I come."

[31] Augustine, *Confessions*, VIII, sec. 12, Christian Classics Ethereal Library https://www.ccel.org/ccel/augustine/confess.ix.xii.html.

A Computable Universe?

In a recent compendium of articles concerning the work of the consummate mathematical theorist and code-breaker Alan Turing, the following appears: "Alan Turing never said that the physical universe is computable, and nor do any of his technical results entail that it is. Some computer scientists and physicists seem infuriated by the suggestion that the physical universe might be incomputable; but it is an important issue, and the truth is that we simply do not know."[1]

Why should there be such a negative reaction on the part of "some computer scientists and physicists"?

Two reasons appear possible. We shall deal with each in turn.

First, the evidence for a completely materialistic, mechanistic (and therefore entirely computable) universe is so powerful that any other approach should be rejected out of hand.

However, it should be obvious that the universe is so vast that no argument asserting that only materialistic explanations are possible must *perforce* fail. At least since Einstein, the universe cannot be regarded as a tight playing field where we humans know all the rules (or can potentially discover them).

But have not the materialists been successful in showing the nonapplicability of "spiritual" claims to explain phenomena? In the realm of spiritualism and professional magic, the successes have

---

[1] Jack Copeland, Mark Sprevak, and Oron Shagrir, "Is the Whole Universe a Computer?," in *The Turing Guide*, ed. Jack Copeland, *et al.* (Oxford: Oxford University Press, 2017), 445–62.

indeed been impressive. The debunking of spirit-explanations has been very important to the history, for example, of the Society for Psychical Research.[2]

The difficulty, however, lies in the welter of phenomena still inexplicable materialistically. One thinks, for example, of the after-death appearances of C. S. Lewis to New Testament scholar and translator J. B. Phillips:

> The late C. S. Lewis, whom I did not know very well and had only seen in the flesh once, but with whom I had corresponded a fair amount, gave me an unusual experience. A few days after his death, while I was watching television, he "appeared" sitting in a chair within a few feet of me, and spoke a few words which were particularly relevant to the difficult circumstances through which I was passing. He was ruddier in complexion than ever, grinning all over his face and, as the old-fashioned saying has it, positively glowing with health. The interesting thing to me was that I had not been thinking about him at all . . . A week later, this time when I was in bed, reading before going to sleep, he appeared again, even more rosily radiant than before, and repeated to me the same message, which was very important to me at the time. I was a little puzzled by this, and I mentioned it to a certain saintly bishop who was then living in retirement here in Dorset. His reply was, "My dear J__ __, this sort of thing is happening all the time."[3]

Even more significant are the considerable number of historical miracle claims *not reasonably capable of materialistic explanation.* Chief among them is the resurrection of Jesus Christ from the dead. We cannot here go into the detailed evidence (it is readily available elsewhere), but we note simply the presence of reliable witnesses (1) to Jesus's death and burial and (2) to his resurrection appearances—of his physical body—during a forty-day period following his crucifixion.[4]

---

[2] See John Warwick Montgomery, *Principalities and Powers: The World of the Occult* (Minneapolis, MN: Bethany, 1973).

[3] J. B. Phillips, *Ring of Truth* (New York: Macmillan, 1967), 118–19.

[4] See Montgomery, *History, Law and Christianity* (3rd ed.; Irvine, CA: 1517 Legacy/New Reformation Press, 2014); and *Christ as Centre and Circumference*

Only one such proof is enough to deep-six a universally applicable materialistic metaphysic.

So—if materialism cannot be established as a universal explanation of things, why become incensed over a noncomputable universe?

To be sure, one might argue that the issue is not in fact *materialism* but *mechanism*: regardless of whether everything is at root material, the universe is a machine and is therefore in principle computable.

Wittgenstein rightly observed that logic (and therefore mathematics and computation) does not show us the substance of the world; it is like the scaffolding of a building—it shows us the "shape" of the world, but not what it consists of.[5] 2 + 2 = 4, but we are not told from the mathematical formula (or by any computer program) what the 2s are: they could be trees—or they could be tooth fairies.

It follows that for a human being to show that the entire universe is computable, he or she would have to demonstrate that it is in fact no more than a machine (the same impossible problem as showing that the universe is nothing but materialistic) *and* that one has arrived at the nature of the cosmic program totally defining it.

Charles Babbage, in arguing for the legitimacy of miracle in a universe of physical laws, used the analogy of a computer that only rarely, and seemingly randomly, produces a strange, apparently miraculous, result. If one knew the complete program, the result would be perfectly understandable—but not otherwise. Babbage was

---

(Bonn, Germany: Verlag fuer Kultur und Wissenschaft, 2012).

[5] *Tractatus Logico-Philosophicus*, 6.124. "The 'scaffolding' of the world (6.124a) is the same as the logical form of the world. In saying that logic exhibits (*darstellt*) this scaffolding, Wittgenstein is reminding us of his point, by now familiar, that logical propositions are concerned only with logical form and so, in a sense, have no subject-matter. Yet he insists that logic nevertheless has a 'connexion' with the world (6.124c), so that although logical propositions are not about the objects of the world, they still 'show something about the world' (6.124d)" (Max Black, *A Companion to Wittgenstein's "Tractatus"* [Cambridge: Cambridge University Press, 1971], 329).

saying that only God possesses the universal program (and thus miracles to us are not miracles to him).[6]

It follows that from a mechanistic point of view, human subjects would not be able to account for miraculous occurrences or be capable of arriving at a complete computational description of the universe. It is therefore irrelevant whether the computabilist is a materialist or a mechanist: in both instances, his *Weltanschauungen* is fideistic, the product of blind faith.

This brings us to the second possible understanding of the "infuriation" produced by a noncomputability viewpoint.

Is it not likely that the computabilist is dreadfully threatened by the reality of a nonmaterialistic, nonmechanistic universe—one that he or she would not, even in principle, be able to explain? It has been said, "God created us in his image, and ever since we have been returning the compliment." That is to say, the self-centered, fallen human race wants to *be God*, and nothing is more irritating than having to admit that that will not work. Human egoism is in permanent tension with human finitude. We want to be God and to be able to explain—compute—everything. But our finitude (and the real history of things) makes this simply a nonoption. So we have a psychological fit or two, and claim that—in spite of all the solid evidence to the contrary—*we really can* in principle explain the entire universe in its amazing complexity and diversity.

Suggestion: Grow up. Maturity consists of recognizing the way things in fact *are*; not endeavoring mythically to turn the universe into the kind of place we would like it to be, centered on ourselves. Freud had it backward (*Moses and Monotheism*): the mythmaking is not on the part of religious believers; it is the mechanistic materialist who mythically creates a world of total computability and explainability that will pander to his or her ego and wish fulfilment.[7]

---

[6] See Montgomery, "Computer Origins and the Defense of the Faith," in *Christ as Centre and Circumference* and in *Perspectives on Science and Christian Faith* 56, no. 3 (September 2004): 189–203.

[7] Permission has been granted from the Editor of *Philosophia Christi* to reprint this article, first published in its Winter, 2017, issue (www.epsociety.org/philchristi).

How *Not* to Interpret the Bible

When my wife and I are in London, we generally attend the church of my Inn of Court. Barristers must be members of at least one of four "Inns"—medieval guilds of lawyers. I am a member of both Middle Temple and Lincoln's Inn. (I was called to the bar at Middle and subsequently joined Lincoln's in part because of its superior wine cellar; but that is another story.) Each Inn has its own church or chapel; they are "Royal Peculiars"—that is, directly responsible to the Queen and not under the authority of the local bishop (in this instance, the Bishop of London). Traditionally, they are—like the barristers themselves—conservative in temperament, using the seventeenth-century *Book of Common Prayer*'s magnificent liturgies.

During the so-called legal long vacation in the summer months, one needs to find another worship location. Close to Ludgate Circus is St. Bride's Church, designed by Christopher Wren after the Great Fire of 1666 and traditionally the church of the journalists (when they inhabited Fleet Street). On the Ninth Sunday after Trinity (August 13, 2017), we attended service there, especially because of the wonderful Choral Eucharist.

The downside was the preacher: the Reverend Canon Alison Joyce, rector of St. Bride's. After it was too late to go elsewhere, I remembered a sermon she had preached some time ago on death, arguing, with no mention of the biblical teaching that death is the product of sin (Romans 3:23) or that Christ is the answer (Romans 6:23), that death is essential to the human race since otherwise the world would be overpopulated and people would still be forced to live even though suffering from the dreadful diseases and pain of extreme old age.

Joyce's sermon on this occasion was an interpretation of Matthew 14:22–33, where our Lord walks on water.

She began—encouragingly—debunking a Florida university professor who claimed that a rational explanation for the event was the extreme climate at the time: ice formations on the Sea of Galilee would have given the impression that Jesus was walking on water.

The rector then followed this with her own brand of rationalism (a rationalism picked up, to be sure, from the literary critics of the New Testament). Said she: We must understand what the Gospel writers were actually doing. They wrote to show how special Jesus was. The feeding of the five thousand was to show that Jesus was infinitely more important that the Old Testament prophet Elisha, who had miraculously fed a small number of people (2 Kings 4:42–44)—and the walking on the water was so much more effective than Old Testament parallels that those hearing the story would have seen the merits of believing in Jesus (cf. Job 9:8).

Moreover, said she, what good would Jesus's actually walking on water be to us today? Whereas Jesus's message to Peter and the other disciples, "Fear not," is available to us right now in our difficulties. The miracle of calming fear and giving us hope takes place all the time in the church and in the lives of believers.

What is going on here?

1. The text is being dehistoricized, in flat disregard of what the Gospel writers say they are doing—namely, presenting the precise facts of Jesus's earthly ministry (Luke 1:1–4; cf. 2 Peter 1:16).

2. A new, unhistorical meaning is being given to the text on the basis of Old Testament parallels. These parallels are, of course, genuine and function as "types" of Christ, but they hardly suggest that the New Testament writers redid the events of Jesus's life in defiance of what actually occurred—to show that he was greater than what one finds in the Old Testament. Moreover, how could they

have gotten away with it? The Gospel materials were in circulation when hostile witnesses of Jesus's ministry were still alive; they would surely have blown the whistle on such falsifications—they had means, motive, and opportunity.

3. If the miraculous event did not in fact occur, why should one accept the spiritual lesson the preacher draws from it? Jesus said, notably, "If I have told you earthly things and you believe not, how shall you believe if I tell you of heavenly things?" (John 3:12).

4. The obvious reason for handling the text as Joyce did is to avoid having to assert and defend the miraculous. But isn't a miraculous Resurrection the very heart of Christian faith, and would we not potentially lose even that if such an interpretive method were forced on the New Testament? Maybe there wasn't a historical, bodily Resurrection at all—maybe the important thing is to see that Jesus is more life-affirming than Old Testament prophets?

Conclusion: The preacher's rationalism is no better, and no more justifiable, than the Florida professor's appeal to ice formations. Indeed, it is far more dangerous, for it provides the ideal opportunity to disabuse ourselves of the factual reality of the saving biblical message—of the factuality of the very Incarnation itself. A God who miraculously created the cosmos out of nothing is surely capable not only of *de facto* virgin births and resurrections but also of *de facto* walkings upon water.

About the Author

Emeritus Professor of Law and Humanities, University of Bedfordshire, England; Professor-at-Large, 1517: The Legacy Project, California, USA; and Director, International Academy of Apologetics, Evangelism and Human Rights, Strasbourg, France (www.apologeticsacademy.eu). Ph.D., Chicago; D.Théol., Strasbourg; LL.D., Cardiff; Dr. [h.c.], Institute for Religion and Law, Moscow. Barrister-at-Law (England and Wales), Avocat à la Cour (Paris), Member of the California, District of Columbia, Virginia, Washington State, and US Supreme Court bars. Dr. Montgomery's legal specialty is the international and comparative law of human rights, and he regularly pleads religious freedom cases before the European Court of Human Rights. He is a dual US and UK citizen, the author of some fifty books in five languages (www .newreformationpress.com), and is included in *Who's Who in America*, *Who's Who in France*, the *European Biographical Directory*, *Who's Who in the World*, and *Contemporary Authors*.